D1766380

Richmond upon Thames Libraries

Renew online at www.richmond.gov.uk/libraries

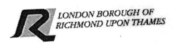
LONDON BOROUGH OF
RICHMOND UPON THAMES

THE
REBEL
SUFFRAGETTE

'With passion and courage, women have taught us that when we band together to advocate for our highest ideals, we can advance our common well-being and strengthen the fabric of our nation.'

President Barack Obama

THE
REBEL
SUFFRAGETTE

THE LIFE OF EDITH RIGBY

BEVERLEY ADAMS

PEN & SWORD **HISTORY**

AN IMPRINT OF PEN & SWORD BOOKS LTD.
YORKSHIRE – PHILADELPHIA

First published in Great Britain in 2021 by
PEN AND SWORD HISTORY
An imprint of
Pen & Sword Books Ltd
Yorkshire – Philadelphia

ISBN 978 1 52677 390 6

A CIP catalogue record for this book is available from the British Library.

Typeset in Times New Roman 11.5/14 by
SJmagic DESIGN SERVICES, India.
Printed and bound by CPI Group (UK) Ltd, Croydon, CR0 4YY

Pen & Sword Books Limited incorporates the imprints of Atlas, Archaeology,
Aviation, Discovery, Family History, Fiction, History, Maritime, Military, Military
Classics, Politics, Select, Transport, True Crime, Air World, Frontline Publishing,
Leo Cooper, Remember When, Seaforth Publishing, The Praetorian Press,
Wharncliffe Local History, Wharncliffe Transport, Wharncliffe True Crime and
White Owl.

For a complete list of Pen & Sword titles please contact
PEN & SWORD BOOKS LIMITED
47 Church Street, Barnsley, South Yorkshire, S70 2AS, England
E-mail: enquiries@pen-and-sword.co.uk
Website: www.pen-and-sword.co.uk

Or
PEN AND SWORD BOOKS
1950 Lawrence Rd, Havertown, PA 19083, USA
E-mail: Uspen-and-sword@casematepublishers.com
Website: www.penandswordbooks.com

MIX
Paper from
responsible sources
FSC® C013604

Contents

Acknowledgements

Writing a book is definitely not a one woman show. There have been a lot of people who have come together to help me get this book to the point it is at now, and I owe them such a debt of gratitude.

Firstly, to my wonderful publisher Pen and Sword History for giving me the opportunity to tell Edith's story. Especially to Jonathan Wright for offering me the chance to write this book, and Aileen Pringle, whose friendliness meant asking the daftest of questions was so much easier. She offered some very encouraging and supportive words way back at the beginning of this journey and has been a point of contact who kept me reassured that everything was ok. Thanks also to my editor, Claire Hopkins, for your patience and for answering my questions, and for offering lots of encouragement and guiding me through this process. I would also like to thank Laura Hirst for all her hard work in bringing everything together.

To my mum and dad for providing me with copious amounts of information about Preston, and for filling in the blanks to explain what the town was like in their younger days. Trying to imagine a Preston different from what I know now was not easy. To my brothers Chris and Paul for instilling in me that Preston North End FC was the club for me; pride in my club instils pride in my city.

To my wonderful friends: firstly, Leona Steel, who really was the person who suffered the most during the early stages of this project. She listened to me talk for a long time about my desire to write a book about Edith, and her encouragement gave me the push I needed and the enthusiasm and excitement when I got the go ahead was fabulous!

My 'Laydeez': Gill Parker, Carol Worster and Pat Palmer – you three are always on hand to provide the laughs, and I do laugh every time we get together. We may be far apart but you are always close by. Lorraine Mawdsley, never have I met a more optimistic and positive person, always on hand to bat away any negative comments. Nothing is an obstacle and there is always a positive spin to be had; she has always said I could do it,

Acknowledgements

and she was right. Kathryn Baxendale, thank you for joining me on my research schlep around Preston and for reading snippets throughout the process, I royally thank you for your time and encouragement; despite not knowing you for that long I consider you to be a very good buddy.

Finally, the best of them all is Emma Powell. She provides everything I need when I need it: support, encouragement, reassurance, understanding, many, many laughs and the best scrambled eggs known to man. Never have I met someone as kind, thoughtful and generous as you and I consider myself extremely lucky to call you my friend. Out of all my friends I think you are the one who embodies Edith's spirit the most – her determination, kindness and ability to sort out any tricky situation with a calm head.

Lots of thanks go to all my wonderful colleagues who have been with me all the way, in particular to my good pal Marie Drelincourt for the endless support, belief and archive trips; Chris Smith for your endless ability to tell it like it is and the reminders of what I am actually capable of and Gary Huzzey for dropping fascinating little bits of inspiration my way. Lots of thanks to Lisa, Liz, Lynn, Win, Tracey and Nicky for reassuring me that I could do it, and to all of you who have taken an interest and listened, encouraged and supported me from the start. A special thank you to Chris Summerton, sadly no longer with us, but he always said I would write a book and I have proved him right. I know if he was still with us he would have been so pleased that I had achieved my dream.

Thank you to all the wonderful women who very kindly offered to take part in my suffragette survey. I am eternally grateful to you for taking the time to give thoughtful and considered answers and for being honest in your views. To all the wonderful bookish friends that I have made on Twitter for your excitement and reassurance. Even though we have never met in person, you have provided me with some essential pick me ups when I have needed them, and some cracking book recommendations!

Immense thanks go to the wonderfully talented Catherine Curzon, this book would almost certainly not have happened if she had not reached out and offered me some much-needed guidance and advice. The kindness of a stranger gave me the hope and determination that my dream could in fact become a reality, and if I am half as good a writer as you I will be very happy.

Thank you to the patient people at the Lancashire Archives for trawling through various documents and papers, and to the wonderful people at

The Friends of Winckley Square organisation for providing such a wealth of material and for the kindness you showed me at one of your talks on Edith; I was having a writing wobble but I left walking on air.

This book definitely could not have been written without the information provided by Phoebe Hesketh in her book *My Aunt Edith*. Edith did not leave a lot of information about herself behind, there are not many pictures or stories of her life so this resource has been utterly valuable. I am very conscious that my book is not simply a retelling of her work and I hope I have given my own voice to Edith's life story and I thank her for giving me Edith's words to work from. A thank you goes to all the wonderful female writers that have written about the suffragettes over the years, your knowledge is phenomenal and one day I hope I can achieve the level of success you all have.

Even though I cannot actually offer her my thanks, I must say a huge thank you to Edith Rigby herself. When I discovered Preston had its own suffragette I was intrigued, but I never imagined I would go on the journey I did. I am proud to call her a fellow Prestonian and I feel privileged to walk the streets she once did. I knew she was my kind of woman when I learnt she had lobbed a black pudding at an MP; you can take the girl out of Lancashire…

Finally, the biggest thank you must go to all those women, whether suffragette or suffragist, militant or peaceful campaigner, for fighting so hard and so bravely so that women like myself can vote freely and safely today. We are very grateful for all the sacrifices you made to ensure we had our freedom to have our say.

Preface

The thought of writing a book about any topic was nothing but a pipe dream to me about seven years ago. I had just graduated with an English Literature degree from the Open University and was about to embark on my Master's degree, also with the OU; three years later I graduated and I needed to put it to good use.

I cannot actually pinpoint when my interest in the suffragettes began. I have always been a lover of history so I imagine the topic came up on a documentary at some point and it went from there. They had always been somewhat of a myth to me – I knew what they did and what they stood for, but I was fascinated to see these women smashing the windows of shops in London, chaining themselves to railings at Downing Street and basically causing all out mayhem. But, the most overriding image that hooked me in was the tragic death of Emily Wilding Davison at the Epsom Derby in 1913. She was struck by the king's horse as it rounded the last bend and I thought to myself, 'why did she do that?' Was what she was fighting for really that important? Well yes, as it turns out, it was. The first time I watched the newsreel of that most horrific moment just struck me dumb, I knew I needed to investigate further and when I discovered they were fighting for the right to vote it came as a shock. I had always been able to vote, as had my mother and grandmother, 'so hadn't women always been able to vote?' I thought to myself. Evidently not.

Shortly after graduating with my MA I watched the film *Suffragette* and again it awoke something in me, the story of the main character is heartbreaking. She has to decide whether to fight for her rights as a woman or risk losing her home and child. I couldn't actually believe that this had happened and that women were put in these situations. I had known of Emmeline Pankhurst from an early age, but when I discovered that my home town of Preston had its very own suffragette, who was fully engaged in the campaign for 'Votes for Women', I decided it was time to delve further.

Spurred on by a new-found confidence to write a lengthy piece of work and with a topic to research, I decided I was going to write a book about my own local suffragette. Being a Prestonian, I have always taken a keen interest in those from my home town who have made it big, and to find that Edith had been a black-pudding-throwing suffragette with a penchant for paraffin made her an irresistible subject. We should not condone the violence used by the suffragettes, although it is hard not to admire their sheer guts and determination to fight for their rights and that is one of the things I admire most about them. But in Edith I had found a Lancashire lass who, just like me, felt the injustices towards women needed action. Edith was very relatable to me. I walk the same streets she did, I can visit the building she was born in, the church she got married in and the grand Georgian townhouse she lived in, I felt like I was holding my hand out to the past and she was reaching from the other side. Her birthplace of Preston has recognised her importance with Edith Rigby House and a commemorative blue plaque on the walls of 28 Winckley Square, although we are still awaiting the statue that the council had previously tried to erect.

I knew early on that Edith was going to be like no woman I had come across before, but then you had to have something about you to endure the things she did. I went on guided walks around Preston taking in the Edith Rigby sights, I sat in the archives trying to piece together the very few fragments of details she left behind and spent many an hour using online family research resources in an attempt to piece together her family tree. She has an extensive family and there are some interesting stories to be had there, but I do not feel it is my place to go raking up family secrets – my book is about her known life and her career as philanthropist and suffragette. There are many layers to Edith Rigby and I feel I have only scratched the surface, unfortunately for me she did not like having her picture taken so the number of photos is limited. I would love to have been able to sit down with her to discuss her life for she led a fulfilling and varied life, and one that was ever eventful. I think it is safe to say there was never a dull moment with Edith!

So, after much pondering and deliberation, and after copious amounts of discussions with a friend, I decided that I wanted to tell Edith's story and place her amongst the wider suffragette history. I feel her story is one worth telling, every single woman that was part of the women's suffrage movement deserves her story to be told and I hope I have done Edith the justice she deserves.

Beverley Adams
August 2020

Timeline of Events

December 1809	Birth of William Ewart Gladstone in Liverpool. He was to be prime minister over four terms between 1868 and 1894. He would extend the franchise for more men but still continued to dismiss women.
August 1832	Mary Smith presents Henry Hunt MP with the first women's suffrage petition that was to be presented to Parliament.
September 1852	Birth of Herbert Henry Asquith, in Morley, Yorkshire. He was to be prime minister (1908–1916) and the suffragette's biggest enemy.
August 1856	Birth of Keir Hardie in Lanarkshire, Scotland. He was the founder of the Labour Party and supporter of women's rights.
July 1858	Birth of Emmeline Pankhurst (*née* Goulden) in Manchester.
January 1863	Birth of David Lloyd George in Chorlton-on-Medlock, Manchester. As prime minister (1916–1922), he would grant partial voting rights to women.
June 1866	John Stuart Mill MP presents Parliament with the first mass women's suffrage petition. It contained in excess of 1,500 signatures.
January 1867	Across Britain many branches of the National Society for Women's Societies are formed.
May 1867	John Stuart Mill MP fails in his attempt to amend the Second Reform Bill.
April 1868	The first ever public meeting regarding women's suffrage is held at the Free Trade Hall in Manchester.
December 1870	Women win the right to own their own property and money with the passing of the Married Women's Property Act.

October 1872	Edith Rayner is born to Dr Clement Rayner and his wife Mary Pilkington Sharples at 1 Pole Street, Preston, Lancashire.
October 1877	Birth of Teresa Billington-Greig in Preston, Lancashire.
September 1879	Birth of Annie Kenney in Oldham, Lancashire.
September 1880	Birth of Christabel Pankhurst in Old Trafford, Manchester.
September 1893	Edith Rayner marries Dr Charles Rigby at the Lune Street Wesleyan Chapel in Preston, Lancashire.
December 1894	Married and single women are given the right to vote in local elections with the passing of the Local Government Act.
1897	Led by Millicent Fawcett, the National Union of Women's Suffrage Societies (NUWSS) is formed.
February 1900	The Labour Party is formed.
1902	Textile workers from across the north of England present a petition to Parliament demanding votes for women. It contains over 37,000 signatures.
October 1903	The Women's Social and Political Union (WSPU) is formed at 62 Nelson Street, Manchester, the home of Emmeline Pankhurst.
1905	The motto 'Deeds not Words' is used for the first time by the WSPU. This marks the start of their militant campaign.
February 1907	In a rally organised by the NUWSS, over 3,000 women march from Hyde Park to Exeter Hall. This becomes known as the 'Mud March' due to the weather conditions.
	Edith Rigby joins many other WSPU members at Caxton Hall for the first 'Women's Parliament'. They walk to the Houses of Parliament where scuffles break out. Edith is arrested and imprisoned for the first time.
March	The Women's Enfranchisement Bill is presented to The House for a second reading but is talked out. Members of the WSPU attempt to enter the Houses of Parliament, many are arrested.

August	The Qualification of Women Act is passed, allowing women to be elected as councillors and mayors. Founding of the Women's Freedom League by Teresa Billington-Greig and Charlotte Despard. Many suffragettes leave the WSPU, unhappy at the strict running of the organisation, to join them.
February 1908	Edith Rigby is arrested and imprisoned for a second time following further marches on the Houses of Parliament.
June	The largest ever political demonstration in London is organised by the WSPU when 250,000 people attend a rally in Hyde Park. When Asquith ignores their requests, the suffragettes begin smashing windows in Downing Street and attaching themselves to the railings. This became known as Women's Sunday.
July	Mrs Humphrey Ward establishes the Women's Anti-Suffrage League (WASL).
July 1909	Marion Wallace Dunlop becomes the first suffragette to go on hunger strike while in prison. The WSPU adopt this as a new strategy.
September	Force feeding begins on all suffragettes on hunger strike while in prison.
October	The Women's Tax Resistance League (WTRL) is formed and they adopt the motto 'No vote, no tax'. Princess Sophia Duleep Singh becomes a member.
December	Along with three others, Edith Rigby is arrested in Preston following the visit of Winston Churchill. She is released from prison when her father and brother pay her fine. Edith Rigby is arrested and imprisoned following an attack on a Liverpool police station.
August 1910	The WASL and the Men's National League for Opposing Women's Suffrage merge, bringing together approximately 42,000 members.
November	The Conciliation Bill is passed in the House of Commons, but fails to become law. This would have granted suffrage to over a million women who owned property over the value of £10. The suffragettes march

on Westminster to demonstrate but are met with police brutality and it becomes known as Black Friday.

June 1911   Women up and down the country refuse to take part in the census, their argument being if I don't count, then I won't be counted. Many attend parties and walks through London.

November   Following the announcement of the Manhood Suffrage Bill, the WSPU organise a window smashing spree across London. Edith Rigby is arrested and imprisoned.

March 1912   The Parliamentary Franchise (Women) Bill is presented to The House but is defeated by 222 votes to 208.

The Labour Party is the first political party to include female suffrage in their manifesto.

April 1913   Prisoners (Temporary Discharge for Ill Health) Act is introduced. This became widely known as the Cat and Mouse Act. It allowed the release of prisoners on hunger strike only to re-arrest them when they had regained their strength. This continued until the sentence had been served.

June 1913   Emily Wilding Davison is killed when she steps out in front of the king's horse at the Epsom Derby. Thousands attend her funeral.

June-July   The NUWSS organises the Pilgrimage for Women's Suffrage at Hyde Park. Over 50,000 people attend the peaceful rally.

July   Edith Rigby plants a small explosive in Liverpool and later commits arson at Lord Lever's bungalow in Rivington. She gives herself up and is sentenced to nine months in prison.

December   Princess Sophia Duleep Singh faces court action over her refusal to pay taxes.

May 1914   Emmeline Pankhurst attempts to present a petition to King George V at Buckingham Palace, this leads to skirmishes between the WSPU and police.

The NUWSS surpasses 50,000 members while the WSPU reaches 5,000.

July	The outbreak of the First World War sees all campaigning suspended and women turn their attentions to helping the war effort, bringing mass employment to women.
September 1915	Keir Hardie dies in Glasgow. Edith and Charles Rigby buy Marigold Cottage.
1916	Asquith finally acknowledges women's enfranchisement and declares his allegiance to the cause.
February 1918	The Representation of the People Act is passed giving women over the age of 30 and men over the age of 21 the right to vote, although women must be married to or be a member of the Local Government Register.
November	The end of the First World War. The Parliamentary Qualification of Women Act is passed, which allows women to stand as MPs. Constance Markiewicz becomes the first female MP to be elected, but as a member of Sinn Fein she declines to take her seat at Westminster.
November 1919	Nancy Astor becomes the first female MP in Britain to take her seat in the House of Commons.
July 1926	Death of Dr Charles Rigby, Edith relocates to North Wales.
February 1928	Asquith dies in Berkshire.
July 1928	The Representation of People Act finally grants women the same voting rights as men (anyone over the age of 21).
May 1929	Women aged over 21 cast their votes in their first General Election. Ramsey MacDonald's Labour Party regain power.
July 1950	Edith Rigby dies at home in North Wales.

Introduction

We have come to know the fight of the suffragettes well over the past 100 years. It was a battle between citizen and state that was well documented and covered in the nation's press both at the time and now. The images of them being arrested and manhandled by the police are well known, their speeches famous for their passion and the tri-colour of purple, green and cream are synonymous with the fight for women's rights across the world. The names of Pankhurst, Kenney and Davison conjure images of women with ardent and determined looks on their faces. The moving pictures of women dressed in white marching through the streets of London, proudly carrying their arrowed poles denoting their time spent in prison are much watched. They were women who were not frightened by the fight or kowtowed into submission, and after every knock they got back up and they got back up stronger and more determined to succeed.

As the fight for suffrage raged across the globe, it was the suffragettes in this country that brought the government to heel. It was not pretty and at times it was a very unfair and distressing fight, but the women of the United Kingdom united against its leaders to demand the right to vote. They had asked politely in the past and in turn had been politely fobbed off, so it was time to pack away the good manners and to start fighting tough.

There had been many times in the country's history when women had tried to raise their collective voice against the authority of man, but they had not been very successful, most of them had never been powerful enough to overcome man's hold on them, but the country was changing and so were they. The discussion of women's rights was starting to become widespread, so they had a new-found confidence and felt that now was the right time to strike. It was time that the fusty, self-important men of Westminster be brought to heel, it was time they listened to what these women were saying. They were to be ignored at the government's own risk. Initially it was a risk the government were willing to take for the earlier protests went nowhere, but at each set back the women cranked up the ferocity of their campaigning to another level until they reached a point of pure militancy, where no public property was out of bounds to attack and no politician was safe from lobbying.

The discussion surrounding women's rights and their campaign to win the right to vote dominated the nineteenth and early twentieth century. It became a period in the country's history that saw a huge social shift away from the elitist government to a more democratic approach, but women needed to fight to be part of that approach. More and more men were being granted enfranchisement while women of all classes were being left behind with no voice and no representation. Setback after setback left women feeling angry and vulnerable, so they decided it was their time to take matters in to their own hands and to start the fight back.

Initially a peaceful fight, it turned more violent in the early twentieth century when the Pankhurst family from Manchester decided to form a suffrage movement that would become famous not only in this country, but throughout the world. They were to become symbols of hope for supressed women everywhere as they provided a focal point for a campaign to finally win women the vote, they used catchy slogans and held rallies across the country in an attempt to enlist more women to their ranks. The many women that joined them on this quest were fearless and brave, they accepted the risks of imprisonment and some were even willing to give their lives for the cause, for the cause was much greater than they ever could be. It was an incredibly selfless fight for they were not just fighting for themselves but for all the future generations of women who would go to the polling stations with a little bit of the Pankhurst spirit in them. They were under no illusions that the battle was going to be an easy one for many had tried and failed before them, it would be no easy feat to take on the government of one of the world's most powerful countries and come out victorious. But they were prepared and they had plans. They also had each other, and the bond and spirit among them was rock solid; this was quite clearly going to be a fight until the finish.

The battle lines had been drawn when the government had previously declined to hold any serious discussions about the prospect of women getting the vote. They had never given any credence to women having the vote, it was seen as a ridiculous idea and one that ought not to be entertained. Acknowledgement of these women was to concede they had a point and that they should be listened to, which was one thing the government were not willing to do. As it turned out this was to be something far bigger than either of the two rival factions could ever have imagined, and that it would be the biggest battle of all which would bring its end.

At the start of the First World War the focus shifted to uniting to help the country survive. It was time for the women of the United Kingdom to cease their campaign and to collaborate for a greater cause, a cause that would help feed the nation and keep it on an even footing when the men were away fighting in the trenches on the front line. The women that the country now relied upon were the very ones who had been callously dismissed as unimportant and unvalued by the government not that long before; they were ones who had been starved in prison just months ago. However, now they became so important that the country could not have survived without them. Not only were they helping to keep the country going but they had also suffered the agony of sending their husbands, sons and brothers off with good wishes and a prayer for a safe return. The heartache that must have caused we can only imagine, but they had to put that to one side and carry on.

These women were the epitome of courageous and heroic, if at times a little reckless and foolhardy, and made the conscious decision that no act of militancy was out of bounds, as long as it caused no physical harm to any person. They were arsonists, bombers, vandals and downright militant, but they were committed to their cause. It took a special kind of woman to join their ranks but many flocked to their speeches and rallies and raised their banners in protest. Edith Rigby, a doctor's wife from Preston, joined their ranks and was to experience the full force of the campaign. She never shied away from a challenge and served her time in prison with pride and satisfaction that she had helped the cause. Edith was just one of these special women that made it possible for women today to vote, they all stood up to be counted and faced their enemy head on. They were game changers; they were the suffragettes.

Chapter One

The Early Campaigns

On 14 December 1918, women over the age of 30 who met the voting criteria of either owning property, or having a husband who did, were finally allowed to cast their vote in a General Election in the United Kingdom. They had been granted the vote when the Representation of the People Act was passed by the government earlier that year. This meant that over 8.5 million women were now eligible to vote, and when the time came they went to the polling stations with smiles on their faces and a spring in their step, for they could hardly believe that historic day had finally arrived. Despite this huge leap forward for women's rights, it would be another ten years before the franchise was fully extended to all women on the same terms as men, but for those casting their vote in 1918 it had been a hard-fought victory. The victory of the 'Votes for Women' campaign had been a long drawn-out affair between the majority of women and the government, it was a time when the women of the United Kingdom banded together across the four nations to demand that the time had come to rip up the social handbook and accept that women, just like men, were an important and integral part of society and the country as a whole. They had had enough of being typecast as the homemakers and family carers. Women wanted change, they wanted to have their voices heard by the people that mattered; they wanted an opportunity to be counted and to feel counted. They wanted the vote and they were going to make sure they got it!

It was during the early Victorian period that the gender gap in society across the UK was the widest it had ever been. In times before this you may have seen women working alongside men within the family business, whether that was in a provisions store, apothecary or some other type of establishment. It may even have been within the home producing goods that were then sent out to be sold. Regardless of the actual role, there was a place for women within the working sphere. However, the Victorian era saw the dawn of the Industrial Revolution and before long the cottage industry was gone and big industrial factories and textile mills started to appear in towns and cities right across the country. New inventions meant that manufacturing was possible on a much larger scale with a greater profit yield for the factory owners. It also meant more employment opportunities. The decline of the cottage industry forced families to seek work in these factories, so men started to travel to their place of work, and with a more stable and larger income the women could be left behind to tend solely to the domestic side of life. We were at a point in history when specific tasks became either for men or women. The man was expected to go out to work to earn the money to provide for his family, it was seen as his responsibility to put food on the table and to keep a roof over their heads. For the woman, well, it was her job to ensure that food was cooked and on the table for whenever the man of the house required and to tend to the children or elderly relatives. She was also expected to keep the house clean and tidy and ready for any potential guests that decided to visit, it was her responsibility to entertain them and to make sure they had refreshments. She may also have taken in extra work in the evening such as sewing or the mending of garments on behalf of local businesses. Working class women did not have a lot of leisure time to relax; their role was a busy one and their days were long. Of course, we are looking at a certain level in society here – if you were poor and staring poverty in the face then you went out to work regardless of your gender and you did whatever work you could get. A poor man did not have the luxury of being able to leave a wife at home to take care of the domestic arrangements, and she certainly did not have the luxury of just focusing on the domestic side of life. The woman of a poorer household would have to do her domestic chores when she got in from work, for the lot of a poorer woman was to contribute financially and to ensure the tea was cooked and the house kept clean. If the woman was single then she may have entered service in a grand house and become a servant waiting on the needs of the rich, but that did provide her with a small income and a roof over her head. These hard-working families were grateful for the employment they had. They may not have liked it and felt they deserved more in terms of pay and benefits, but they were the lucky ones – the next rung down on the social ladder would have seen them in the workhouse, where couples were split up and children taken from their parents. But here in lies the groundwork for the suffrage movement, as it is important to remember that these women were going to work in the mills and factories, putting in a hard day's work just as the men did, but they were not enjoying the same privileges: they could not vote in the General Election, and their voices were not heard. Without that, things could never change for them. That being said, *no* woman could vote. Society may have differentiated between men and women, but it did not differentiate between women. All women were seen as the same, and working women were barred from having the vote just as much as the ladies who sat in their drawing rooms taking tea with their companions in the afternoon. No woman at any level of society was considered worthy enough of having the vote; they were all considered to be irresponsible.

Queen Victoria sat at the head of the British Empire, it was progressive and led the way in many areas of innovation, which began in the UK with the onset of the Industrial Revolution. Despite this, they did lag behind some nations when it came to giving women the vote and the queen did little to support the cause. 'What right', she thought, 'did they have to assume the role of men?' Yes, she was the ruler of the whole empire, very much seen as a male role, but her role as a monarch was because of birth right, not because she had outwitted, bested or been promoted ahead of any man. In earlier times female monarchs were under constant threat from male family members, who may have held a lower rank but that would have been overlooked if it meant they could displace a woman. For example, Elizabeth I knew she could not marry, if she did then her husband would have assumed power over her, both within the marriage and also in terms of governance, as women were expected to obey their husbands in all matters. She also feared that being married could have led to her having a son and her advisors would have preferred an infant child on the throne rather than a woman. In the end Elizabeth decided she would not risk any threat to her power and announced that she was married to her country, becoming known as the Virgin Queen. Despite being queens, Elizabeth, Victoria and all the other female monarchs who have sat on the throne of the United Kingdom have been surrounded by a host of powerful men who were only too eager to advise, for surely they knew what was best for the country, not a female sovereign.

The working conditions of women and their lack of representation at any level formed the basis of a movement that began to swell across the nation. In the mid-nineteenth century the campaign for women's suffrage began to grow, taking hold in Britain as the 'Votes for Women' campaign, which would become a tidal wave of attack against the Liberal government. Before any of that could happen they needed a platform and a vehicle to peddle their campaign, so a group of like-minded women decided to band together for the common cause and demand change. The movement initially started out as a peaceful protest led by a group of respectable middle-class ladies, whose main aim was to raise awareness to the plight of women. They wanted to bring into the public consciousness the argument that it was high time for change, and that it was their intention to challenge Parliament as such. It was to be considered a dignified and proper campaign which was to be undertaken in a law-abiding, peaceful and calm manner and in the utmost respectful way.

In December 1884 William Gladstone introduced the Third Reform Act and later the Redistribution Act (in which it was agreed the franchise would be extended to include not only towns and cities but also the countryside), which meant if a man paid £10 in rents, or he held his own land worth over £10, he was now entitled to vote. The Redistribution of Seats Act 1885 looked to redraw the boundary lines in towns and cities and out in the rural areas. The aim was to ensure that there was a fair distribution of electoral districts, meaning each district would have at least one member of Parliament, although in twenty-three districts it returned more than two. With the implementation of these Acts more men were granted the vote. The small ruling elite was becoming a thing of the past as a more democratic and representative Parliament was being formed, but it still continued to exclude women and it was due to this latest snub that women decided the time was right to start a fight back.

The introduction of the act allowed more agricultural workers an opportunity to cast their vote. They had finally been given a voice by the government, and why not? After all, they worked and paid taxes like other men did, so it was only fair that they did too. The introduction of the act also increased the voting populace significantly to approximately 5.5 million, but there was still scope for women to be added to their numbers. The sense of injustice that women felt at the implementation of these Acts caused an outcry and added fuel to the already simmering fire, which spurred many women into finally standing up to fight for the vote. For many of them, it was difficult to comprehend why a man of a lesser social standing and of lesser fortune than herself should have a say in how the country was run, especially as some of those women paid more in taxes, abided by the same laws and contributed to the country's economy just as much as the men did, so why should they not have the vote too? It is a very reasonable question to ask, but – unfortunately for them – women simply did not exist in the eyes of the government, they were invisible citizens who were deemed to have nothing to contribute to society or to the country as a whole.

The hypocrisy of the government knew no bounds. They were happy to take a woman's money in the form of taxes due, but they were unwilling to give her a voice in return for that payment. To them, she was of no worth and her thoughts and ideas were especially to be scoffed at. After all, what reasonable and sensible ideas would any woman have to contribute to the country? Women, it was thought, were run by their emotions and were liable to fall to pieces in an emotional rage should she encounter any difficulties. But the only rage women were experiencing was the downright refusal of the government to give them a voice that would let them be heard, but then maybe the governing few were scared of what they might say, or, that women might actually surprise them and pose considered and well thought-out arguments. The government would not have known how to react if they had come across a group of women who put across their thoughts in a rational and reasonable way.

It was a firmly held belief among the majority of politicians that even if women were to be granted the vote then surely, being the true and proper female ideal, they would just vote how their husbands or fathers had told them to. Would they be foolish enough to defy them and attempt to make their own decision? Politics was a male-dominated arena, and women had no rights getting themselves involved in it. In the eyes of men, women were deemed incapable of making such an important decision for themselves; they were clearly devoid of any sense and unable to take into consideration the various manifestos to make an informed and balanced decision based on the information available. Surely this was beyond their understanding, so they must seek the advice of the greater men in their lives. Was the government really that short-sighted and ignorant to think that women would just meekly comply with this? Admittedly, before the rise of the female suffrage movement, women had displayed behaviour of compliance and duty, there were very few women who went against the grain of society, and if she did she was quite often the lone voice who was quickly quietened. There are a few exceptions to this, but on the whole women were under the control of men. That being said, with the emergence of the various suffrage groups did they honestly think women would continue to be quietened by these reasons? Quite clearly they did, and they were obviously not prepared for the backlash that was to come from these meek, mild and previously compliant citizens. It was quite naïve on the part of the government. For years women had been asking peacefully to be heard and time and time again they ignored their pleas, it was not a shock that they would then try a different plan of attack. The time had now come for women to fight back and prove they were, in fact, just as capable and dependable as men, and that they could be trusted to make an informed decision – but it was precisely these decisions the political parties were frightened of.

The Liberal Party was led by Herbert Henry Asquith, who served as Prime Minister from 1908 to 1916. He was growing increasingly concerned that the trade unions and newly formed Labour Party were beginning to pose too much of a threat, and the fact that the suffragists had started to win them over meant he needed to make a decision. He initially supported the campaign, but when he really thought about it he decided the risk was too great. His party seemed at odds with itself. Some members seemed to support extending the franchise but would then change their mind once the process had started, and the indecision they showed frustrated the women as they never knew how close or, indeed, how far they were from being successful.

Asquith considered the whole enfranchisement of women in terms of the effect it would have on the running of government and whether or not it would aid him in doing so. He gave little credence to the actual rights of women, to him that was not a factor to be considered and he did not understand why women were up in arms about their lack of vote. It was his and his government's inability to make a firm stance one way or the other that caused the women to give up on any chance of winning the vote through peaceful methods. Once the campaigning took on a more militant turn, he quickly changed his mind and decided to oppose any future bill, and the Liberal Party took a hard line against the women from then on. Why Asquith was so indecisive is unclear. On the one hand, many of his party supported women's suffrage and he himself was not against it, but something played on his mind. He believed it was against public opinion and like any other prime minister before him, the main aim of his career was to stay in power, so perhaps it was fear that prevented him forcing the issue through Parliament. That fear came from either upsetting the public, or the fact that if the women were granted the vote, they could potentially vote against him and his party at the first possible opportunity. Surely the latter fear was a misguided notion by Asquith. If the Liberal government had allied themselves with the campaign, it was a very real possibility that the women of the various organisations involved could have voted in his favour and secured his place in government for longer. Either way, at that point he turned his back on the women and instead entered in to an all-out war, making himself a personal target in a campaign that would far exceed what he or the country thought possible.

In 1865 groups of women from across the country decided to come together in branches which cumulatively became known as the Women's Suffrage Committee. They managed to gather over 1,500 signatures as part of a petition that demanded women be given the vote on the same terms as men. The petition for women's suffrage was then handed to two pro-universal suffrage MPs. The first was Henry Fawcett, MP for Brighton, and secondly John Stuart Mill, MP for City and Westminster. Hopes were riding high that finally a breakthrough would be made as an amendment was written into the second Reform Bill of 1867. Unfortunately, when it came to the crunch it was defeated in Parliament by 196 votes to 73. Bitterly disappointed by this latest setback, but sensing that victory was possible, the women decided to take a more structured approach to campaigning and so together they formed women's suffrage committees. When subsequent bills were rejected by Parliament they made the decision that seventeen of these committees would merge together, and in 1897 the National Union of Women's Suffrage Societies (NUWSS) was formed, led by Millicent Fawcett. Millicent spoke publicly on a regular basis about women's rights and was often found in the Ladies' Gallery in the House of Commons listening to the debates; she was also the wife of Henry Fawcett MP. The formation of the NUWSS brought about an organisation which was much more professional and concentrated in its approach; it gave women a focus and one umbrella to campaign under.

This first group of women became known as the suffragists and they believed in peaceful campaigning methods. It was their hope that by using education and a well-constructed argument, they could persuade the government that votes for women was not only a sensible and reasonable suggestion, but one that should be implemented. The lobbying techniques used by the suffragists were moderately successful in that they achieved yearly debates on the issue of women's right to vote, which kept the issue in the public's conscience and kept the discussions relevant. They purposefully chose to lobby the politicians they knew already had sympathetic views towards female suffrage, and it was important to avoid any confrontation so they opted to write directly to MPs, produce leaflets, pamphlets and posters to raise awareness for their cause. The NUWSS consisted mainly of middle- to upper-class women and it was for these women they campaigned for. By 1914 there were approximately 54,000 members and it was the largest of all the women's suffrage groups, but as time went on, and as more of their campaigns ended in disappointment, it was quite clear that for all their peaceful negotiations they had made very little progress, and for some members it was time to take the campaigning to the next level. From that point on it became a much more focused and militant fight that put a whole new group of women in direct conflict with the government. These were women who were not scared to be bold and controversial; many of them came from the textile mill towns of the north who had more to fight for than just having the vote.

In 1903, at 62 Nelson Street in Manchester, Emmeline Pankhurst and her daughters Christabel and Sylvia formed the Women's Social and Political Union (WSPU). They would later become known as the suffragettes, and it did not take long for women to flock to their cause and for branches to be formed up and down the country. There were many differences between the NUWSS and the WSPU, mainly the level of ferocity in their campaigning methods and the size of each organisation, with the NUWSS being the larger of the two but with the WSPU having a much bigger impact. The main difference was that the members of the WSPU were predominantly working-class women who were not frightened to engage in a more militant approach. After all, these women were earning a wage, a hard wage in fact as the conditions in many of the mills were far from salubrious, but they did it to support their families. They were paying their taxes to the government so felt they had every right to have a say in how the country was being run, but in order to do that they needed the vote. They were not scared to commit arson, chain themselves to railings and cause widespread disruption to hammer home their message to those in power.

They were going to make sure their message was heard loud and clear, and they were soon front-page news. Many newsreels were taken at the time which show us the sheer numbers involved in their demonstrations, and soon enough the suffragettes were using the media to their own advantage. They even turned the term 'suffragette', which was initially used by a journalist from the *Daily Mail* in 1906 as a derogative term, into their own, which has stood the test of time. It would be safe to say the press, the government and the country as a whole underestimated how passionate and forceful this group of women could be, and they certainly would never had anticipated the levels they were willing to go to for their cause. The courage and strength of these women cannot be overlooked; they committed these actions knowing it would probably lead to their arrest and possible imprisonment. Admittedly, they may not have realised at that stage the barbaric treatment they would face once they were there, but even when it did become apparent they did not give in and they never shied away from what was thrown at them. To these women the cause was paramount, and no amount of force feeding or threats from the government would halt their campaigning. The suffragettes were clever and quickly realised the arrests and subsequent trials were getting them the column inches they needed so they used it all to their advantage. Knowing that the arrest of these women would cause utter scandal, they mobilised this as their propaganda and continued to use it to highlight the campaign for 'Votes for Women' and keep them in the public eye. Any publicity was good publicity as far as the suffragettes were concerned.

Despite the fierce commitment to the cause there was unrest amongst the WSPU, and in 1907 those who were unhappy with the tactics used by the Pankhurst women and their close allies left and formed the Women's Freedom League (WFL). They believed the best way forward was to employ a peaceful law-breaking approach, which included causing disruption, refusing to pay their taxes or joining in the Census. While the NUWSS, WSPUS and the WFL all had their own approaches, they were all women who felt a change in the law was needed, and regardless of which organisation they aligned themselves with, the cause was a joint one: 'Votes for Women'.

Unsurprisingly there were many, including women, who did not support the suffrage cause, so a list was made which outlined the reasons why women having the vote was a reasonable and legitimate request:

Fourteen Reasons for Supporting Women's Suffrage

1. Because it is the foundation of all political liberty that those who obey the Law should be able to have a voice in choosing those who make the Law.
2. Because Parliament should be the reflection of the wishes of the people.
3. Because Parliament cannot fully reflect the wishes of the people when the wishes of women are without any direct representation.
4. Because most Laws affect women as much as men, and some Laws affect women especially.
5. Because the Laws which affect women especially are now passed without consulting those persons whom they are intended to benefit.
6. Because Laws affecting children should be regarded from the woman's point of view as well as the man's.
7. Because every session questions affecting the home come up for consideration in Parliament.
8. Because women have experience which should be helpfully brought to bear upon domestic legislation.
9. Because to deprive women of the vote is to lower their positions in common estimation.
10. Because the possession of the vote would increase the sense of responsibility amongst women towards questions of public importance.
11. Because public-spirited mothers make public-spirited sons.
12. Because large numbers of intelligent, thoughtful, hard-working women desire the franchise.
13. Because the objections raised against their having the franchise are based on sentiment, not on reason.
14. Because to sum all reasons up in one – it is for the common good of all.

Printed by Bradbury, Agnew & Co., Ltd., London and Tonbridge, for the National Union of Women's Suffrage Societies, and Published by them at 25 Victoria Street, S.W.

There are many familiar names that are synonymous with the suffragettes and their cause: the Pankhurst family, Lancashire mill worker Annie Kenney, the redoubtable Charlotte Despard, 'The General' Flora Drummond, the Pethick-Lawrences, who paid many an early prison fine and the tragic Emily Wilding Davison to name but a few. It was a large organisation and each woman had a part to play in her own way. Some of the women did not relish militant action so they made banners to be carried at processional marches, wrote motivational speeches and cheered from the side lines while others did the nitty gritty work, but there were many women who fought tirelessly for the cause. One of these women was Edith Rigby, a doctor's wife from Preston in Lancashire. She was a determined and passionate woman who firmly believed that women had the right to vote on the same basis as men. She believed so earnestly in her cause that she was willing go to prison for it. She joined the Pankhurst women at their home and signed up to become a member of the WSPU in 1906 and started on the campaign trail almost immediately.

The suffragettes soon became known across the country for their civil disobedience and targeted attacks on buildings and politicians. Edith herself became embroiled in many of these attacks and became a leading force when it came to putting herself out there to carry out various attacks. She took part in campaigns both in Lancashire and in London. She broke windows, threw black puddings at politicians and even attempted to detonate a bomb at the Cotton Exchange in Liverpool; she became a fugitive, on the run after the police made attempts to rearrest her. The threat of imprisonment did not deter Edith and her fellow activists, she was incarcerated seven times in total and during those sentences she even endured hunger strikes and had to be force fed. Her solidarity with her fellow suffragettes was strong and nothing could deter Edith from the cause. She experienced ridicule by some members of society for her support of the WSPU, but thanks to the love and support of her husband she remained steadfast and loyal.

The advent of the First World War halted campaigning for many of the suffragette movements as ordered by Pankhurst family. They felt their energies would be better spent in helping with the war effort. While Edith agreed with the need to pull together for the sake of the country, she did not feel it was the best course of action in terms of the suffragette's campaign. In retaliation and direct rebellion to Pankhurst's orders, she created the Preston branch of the Independent WSPU. This, however, does not paint a full and fair picture of Edith's efforts during war time. She became a member of the Women's Land Army and provided much-needed fresh produce to the people of Preston by growing fruits and vegetables in her garden at home to sell at the town's market. She continued in this vein following the end of the war, when the vote was finally won for some women of society. Edith retired to North Wales to live a reclusive but productive life following the death of her beloved husband.

There are so many tales to tell in the life of Edith Rigby – she was charismatic, passionate, ruthless and thoroughly unpredictable. She was someone who rejected the accepted notion of what a woman of her class should be. The way she dressed and the way she ran her household often came under intense scrutiny, but she was independent in mind and spirit and always had courage in her own convictions. As a suffragette, she was just as effective and brave as the Pankhurst women. There were plenty of women like Edith all across the country who wanted change and weren't afraid to fight for it and their stories are largely similar, they all had to have that characteristic of putting themselves beyond their own lives, they had to see what life was like for other women and how life could be should they win the vote. There are many stories of the lives of the lesser-known suffragettes, all of whom deserve to be recognised for the role they played in achieving women's suffrage. I have chosen Edith due to her being a local suffragette, but when I started to look at her life in depth I was astounded at what lengths she had gone to for what she believed in and her unrelenting desire to do what was right. It also raises many questions regarding life for women today. Did what these women fought for still have a resounding impact on the lives of women in twenty-first-century Britain, or do we take for granted our rights and not fully appreciate the dangerous lengths these women went to in order to get women the fundamental right to vote? Was it all chaining themselves to railings, or did it go much deeper than that?

The campaign for women's suffrage was a countrywide movement and transcended all classes, whether you were pro- or anti-suffrage, women being enfranchised sparked discussion and arguments. So, while there are many stories to be told this is Edith's story: one woman from a northern mill town who held within her a deep burning desire to see women from across all works of life be given a voice, a voice that enabled them to have their say on how their country was being run. Unfortunately, they had to fight the might of the government and while they had some support within Parliament, they were going to need to all their strength and bravery to take them on. While what Edith achieved during her life as a suffragette was remarkable, I make no assumption that what she did was any more or any less than other women in her situation. In fact, it is worth noting here that Edith and the others were just doing what they saw as their duty. They did not want recognition or the limelight – after the eventual success of the campaign, we learn that their lives largely went back to normal. Each woman had to have some desire of wanting to help and affect change, otherwise she would not have coped with the demands of being a suffragette. Each one of them had a driving vision to make the world a better place for women, women just like themselves. They knew no one was going to magically wave a wand and women would have the vote all of a sudden, so they knew they were going to have to do it themselves. But finally the opportunity had arisen, the right group of women in the right circumstances were assembled and the fight could begin.

Chapter Two

Edith's Early Life

Edith Rigby (*née* Rayner) was born on 18 October 1872 in the Lancashire mill town of Preston, in the north of England. She is described as having bright blue eyes with yellow-gold hair, and when she was older she was considered to be quite a striking beauty with a strong nose. She was born in to a lower middle-class family; her parents were Alexander Clement Rayner, a popular surgeon to the working-class people of the town, and Mary Pilkington Sharples, who was otherwise known as Polly. The Rayners' marriage seems to have been a long and happy one which provided a stable and comfortable home for their children. The family's first home was a large three-storey property at 1 Pole Street, which is just off Church Street in the centre of the town. The first four of the Rayners' children were born there before the young family later moved across the road to 58 and 59. The house on Pole Street had a dual purpose: it served as Dr Rayner's surgery on the ground level, with the family's living quarters occupying the upper two floors. It could not have been ideal to have your children traipsing through your surgery when you were trying to treat patients. It was a modestly-sized property and would have been considered one of the best on the street, despite its questionable location. The move to the other side of the road enabled the family to keep the home and the surgery separate, I am sure it also provided the growing family much more room to expand in to. Unfortunately, 58 and 59 Pole Street are no longer standing, but number 1 is, so we can picture the kind of home Edith and her family lived in during those earlier years.

Sadly, tragedy was to strike the family while they lived at number 1, when in 1873 the eldest daughter Lucy died after contracting scarlet fever at the age of 2. It is thought she caught the disease after going with her father to the home of one of his patients who already had the infection. As well as the need for more space it must have been a matter of great importance for Dr Rayner to put a clear distinction between his family home and his surgery. He could not risk any more of his young children coming in to contact with his patients, and he required a safe and secure environment in which he could continue to see and treat them. According to the United Kingdom City and County Directory, he was still practising in Pole Street long after the family moved out and continued to hold the premises until his retirement. It was at 58/59 that the remaining three Rayner children were born. Lucy's death made Edith the eldest child and a total of seven were to be born to Dr and Mrs Rayner: Alice was born in 1874, Arthur in 1877, Henry Herbert in 1880, Henrietta in 1883, who sadly passed away in childhood following a prolonged illness (Edith was 18 at the time and the family were devastated by the loss), and finally Harold in 1886.

The home life of the Rayner children would have been a comfortable one, despite the less-than-salubrious area they chose to live. They were a middle-class family living in a working-class area, and this served as an early reminder to young Edith that not everyone had the same level of comfort and luxuries she did. It can be said the Rayner family was quite a prominent one within Preston Society. Alexander's father, Thomas Alexander Rayner, was born in Sheffield in about 1815, and in his role as a Wesleyan minister he moved around the country. In 1842 he and his wife Ann found themselves living in Shropshire and it was here their son Alexander Clement was born. The family eventually moved to Preston when Thomas took the ministerial vacancy at Moor Park Chapel and the family settled on Garstang Road in Fulwood. Sadly, Thomas passed away on 20 July 1885 in Lancaster, meaning he did not have a great amount of time to spend with his grandchildren. While the young Rayner family were relatively comfortable in terms of their income and home, and were middle-class in their values and social standing, they had purposely chosen to live among the poor in an impoverished part of town. Pole Street is in the heart of the town close by the parish church (now Preston Minster), but at this point in Preston's history it was home to some of the poorest families in the town.

At the time of Edith's birth, Preston (now a city) was a bustling market town with a rich history. Known in its earliest days as 'Priest Town', Preston had long been a wealthy prosperous place and was the administrative centre of Lancashire, having its new county hall built in 1882. In 1179 King Henry II granted the town its royal charter and the right to hold a Guild Merchant, and the Preston Guild has been held every twenty years since. Edith and her family would have enjoyed the processions and ceremonies that took place throughout the town – they may even have taken part in them. The town sits right at the heart of the county on the north bank of the River Ribble and is half way between Glasgow and London, meaning geographically it was well placed to witness many key battles in the country's history, including in August 1648 when Oliver Cromwell's forces met with the King Charles II's troops in one of the English Civil War's most decisive battles. The key part of the battle took place at Walton-le-Dale, just outside of Preston, and proved a victorious battle ground for Cromwell and his army. In 1715 a second 'Battle of Preston' was fought and the town was to play host to the final conflict of the first Jacobite Rising, in which the Jacobite army was defeated. At the final uprising in November 1745, Bonnie Prince Charlie chose to rest in Preston on his way south to London. He was to later to rest his army there again on the return journey as they retreated back north to Scotland following a resounding defeat. It is said the people of Preston gave the prince and his army a good reception, the town had a strong Roman Catholic population and the prince knew they would be on his side.

Lying just 30 miles to the north of the big industrial cities of Manchester and Liverpool, and being a large station on the West Coast mainline, meant that Preston's strategic location ensured its position as an integral part of the cotton industry, which grew rapidly throughout Lancashire in the early- to mid-nineteenth century. Prior to the growth of the cotton industry, Preston was considered one of the country's prettiest market towns, with many wealthy Lancastrian families – including the Earl of Derby – choosing to have their town residences there. It was also the centre for the Duchy of Lancaster's legal profession, so it naturally became home to many lawyers who could split their time easily between Preston and the Inns of Court in London. The building of grand Georgian squares like Winckley Square and the wide boulevards of Church Street, lined with mansions, made Preston the place to live for prosperous men and their families. However, the face of Preston was to change dramatically with the coming of the Industrial Revolution and the cotton industry. The grand houses on Church Street were to be bulldozed and replaced with cotton mills and factories, all of which spewed out copious amounts of pollution and grime from their chimneys. Preston has long since been an innovative town. It became the home of teetotalism when Joseph Livesey founded the Preston Temperance Society in 1833, which was a movement that was to become a worldwide concern. It was in

1815 that Preston became the first town outside of London to have gas-powered street lighting; this proved to be a blessing to the many mill owners who now had the power at their fingertips to force longer working hours and increase productivity almost overnight. The new docks were built just off the River Ribble, meaning ships from all over the world could come and trade in the town. Preston was also the gateway to the Pennines and across to Yorkshire. The technological advances that were made in Preston enabled the cotton industry to be incredibly lucrative and successful, and with the economy that it generated it ensured that other areas of trade grew as well. The population of Preston increased rapidly with many workers leaving the surrounding villages to go and try their luck in one of the big industrial mills. But, the mill owners did not pay well. The average male wage was approximately 14 shillings a week, so the workers could only afford the cheaper terraced houses that had started to be built by mill owners in the streets surrounding the factories. This was the Preston that Edith Rayner and her siblings were born in to and lived amongst, and as the working population grew, so did Dr Rayner's medical practice.

Edith's father was a well-respected man in the town, and rather than remain in the comfort of the family home on Garstang Road he decided to set up his surgery where he was needed the most – among the mills and its workers. Working in the big cotton mills was not an easy job, it consisted of long hours and was often fraught with danger as the looms were large, dangerous machines that clacked at high speeds; if you got stuck or trapped, your injuries could be fatal. One of the lesser jobs available, and one that usually went to children, would be to go under the loom to collect pieces of cotton that had come loose. This job was dangerous as it was sometimes done as the loom was still moving – a still loom was not earning any money. I am sure Dr Rayner treated many a person who had sustained injuries following a collision with a loom, or some other piece of equipment, and some of these injuries would have been as severe as losing a limb, which could in turn prove to be fatal. The atmosphere within the mills would have been dank, dusty and incredibly hot, with the noise level being almost unbearable. All the looms would have run at the same time, and these big clacking machines were so loud it would have resulted in many of the workers developing hearing problems later in life. You would also be susceptible to suffering from conditions such as various forms of arthritis after spending all day being bent over the looms, and eye conditions from the darkness of the factories. You also had to watch out for loose clothing catching in the looms, lest you got caught up and dragged across the factory floor. But as a cotton mill worker, one of your biggest problems came from the fibres from the cotton, which would turn in to a fine white dust that hung in the air. Many of the mills had bad ventilation, so the workers were breathing in dust that would attack the lungs and cause coughs and breathing difficulties. If infection set in and was left untreated, it could prove to be fatal. The workers were being exposed to these conditions twelve hours a day, six days a week, so it was little wonder that combined with the poor living conditions, the working-class people of Preston needed men like Dr Rayner to be close at hand.

There is a newspaper report that mentions Dr Rayner attending to the landlord of the Angler's Inn, the local pub on Pole Street, who had collapsed and died on the premises. The article mentions that Dr Rayner had been treating this unfortunate man for an ongoing illness for about a month before he died. So, it was not just the mill workers that he attended to, and he was certainly kept busy. His practice was one of the largest in the borough and he tended to the medical needs of the people of Preston for fifty years at his surgeries on Pole Street and in Fulwood. He also made house calls for those in dire need of his services, whether he came home and talked of his experiences of treating the poor we do not know, but it is reasonable to suggest that Edith picked up some of his stories, which ignited her passion to help when she could. In these pre-NHS days, any medical services you required had to be paid for, but Dr Rayner was a kind and caring man who did much charitable work with the poor. He was, however, a humble man, and was not the type of person who would ever seek praise or reward for his good deeds. This is a trait we would later see in his daughter, as she seems to have inherited the desire to help the poor simply because what they saw and heard caused them grave concern and felt the injustice was too great to be ignored.

In his obituary in the *British Medical Journal*, Dr Rayner is described as a man who was committed to his profession. He started his working day at 8 am and did not finish until gone 9 pm. His dedication knew no bounds, and he never took a day off sick throughout his lengthy career until the two weeks before his death on 25 November 1916 at the age of 74. He was the president of the local branch of the British Medical Association and was described as a man with an unassuming nature, who took enjoyment in reading, history and walking – even climbing to top of Scafell Pike in the Lake District at the grand age of 58. Edith was later to climb Mount Snowden in her fifties, so she clearly inherited her father's love of the outdoors and his never-say-die attitude. He is described as being a quiet man and reserved in his attitudes, but also one with a determined spirit and great strength of mind, which must have served him well considering the working conditions he must have come across during his career. Sadly, it was inevitable that all the hard work and the challenging working conditions would have a negative effect on him in his later years, as he began to display some unpredictable behaviour. He was once caught travelling around Fulwood on the tram wearing nothing but his underwear and a top hat. Edith's relationship with her father was quite clearly one of love and mutual respect. She inherited so many of his good traits and despite him despairing of her in her suffragette years, he must take some of the responsibility for bringing up a daughter with a deep moral sense of what was right and wrong. If we were ever to wonder why Edith was as passionate and determined as she was, we need look no further than her father.

Edith and her younger siblings all had a rebellious streak, but it was her youngest brother Harold in particular that caused most worry for their parents. He was the practical joker in the family which, despite her good sense of humour, Edith found particularly unfunny, and tried to discourage him from performing his tricks. When the family had moved to Fulwood he would squirt passengers on the passing open-top tram with water from a hose pipe that he fed through the attic windows. He also played the classic penny-on-the-floor trick, which he moved along every time someone tried to pick it up. Edith enjoyed a laugh just as much as the next person, in fact she was renowned for her quick wit and wicked sense of humour, but it was never to be at the expense of someone else, it was not in her nature to mock or laugh. As Harold got older, he provided his parents with the conundrum of what his profession was going to be.

His older brothers both showed a talent for the medical profession like their father. The eldest son, Arthur, studied medicine in Manchester and became a well-respected doctor back in Preston, where he performed many medical procedures, including amputations. He was a progressive man who embraced new ideas and ways of thinking, and in 1904 he helped open and run one of the first x-ray departments in the country at Preston Royal Infirmary, where he worked for forty-two years. The development and the ability to use x-ray equipment now gave hope to cases that would have once been considered helpless. It is said he was still performing x-rays well in to his eighties and never took any precautions against the radiation. Dr Arthur Rayner also served as a medical officer during the First World War, serving in the Middle East. Upon his return he went back to work at the hospital, where he was said to be a great advocate of psychiatry. He lived with his family on the exclusive Ribblesdale Place, just off Winckley Square. Younger brother Herbert also became a doctor and had a successful surgery in Manchester; he was also a senior surgeon at Manchester Royal Infirmary.

For Harold, a life in the medical world was not the one for him. After running away from boarding school he was enlisted by his parents into a training regime based in Liverpool with the Royal Navy. It was hoped that this might instil in him a sense of discipline and work ethic, but sadly it didn't and unfortunately he ran away from this as well. Finally, at their wits end, Dr and Mrs Rayner sent Harold back to Liverpool to board the boat to Canada; he had £10 in his pocket and was told to make a new life for himself. Harold certainly does not come across as the kind of lad to be daunted by this, and on his arrival he managed to find work with a Dutch farmer and ended up marrying his daughter. Together they ran their own grain business in Toronto, which they made a huge success of, and their marriage seemed to be a long and happy one. Their son Herbert would eventually come to England to stay with his Aunt Edith to gain an education at an English school, the two would form a strong bond that lasted a lifetime. He would eventually become a member of the Canadian Navy where he would rise to the high rank of vice-admiral. This is a remarkable achievement for any man, but especially so for one whose father's feeble attempts to adapt to navy life failed miserably.

Edith was a very lucky young girl, who from the age of 11 attended the Preston High School for Girls on Winckley Square. This was a fee-paying school and she remained there until 1885 when, at her father's wish, she attended Penrhos College in North Wales until 1890. Prior to her attending Preston High School for Girls, Edith probably would have been educated at home by her mother, alongside her younger sisters. While most of the girls living alongside Edith were taught household tasks and a basic education at home, when they were old enough they would join the older members of the family out at work. Edith had the advantage of being able to attend an actual school that would have focused on her future as a well-respected lady. As a student at high school, Edith would have studied a wide range of subjects including mathematics, history, natural sciences and political economy, alongside other subjects that would have been deemed appropriate for her future role as housewife, including needlework, drawing and singing. It is likely that while she was a student here Edith developed a keen interest in the divisions of class, and how society treated those people on each rung of the society ladder. As a fee-paying school, it is also likely that her classes would have been made up of girls from the lower middle classes upwards. She would not have been mixing with the girls of working-class families that she lived among in Pole Street, and the contrast between the street where she lived and the grand opulent Georgian square where she attended school must have raised some questions for the young Edith. It was her education at school, and later at college, which first lit the torch for equality and fairness for all within Edith; all she had to do was wait for the right opportunity and the means with which she could take action to ignite it fully.

Following her time at the high school she left home to attend boarding school. Penrhos College was a girls-only Methodist school situated just above the promenade in Rhos-on-Sea; the close proximity to the sea shaped Edith's later life and her love affair with North Wales. Her life as a student at Penrhos College was fulfilling, and it was here that she met her lifelong friend Annie Taylor. Annie was a far more vivacious person than Edith, and when Annie discovered boys it was Edith's straight mind and character that showed Annie how she was wasting the privileged opportunity she had been provided by her family. It is not that Edith was a prude – far from it – but like Preston High School, Penrhos College was a fee-paying school, and she was conscious of the fact that her hard-working father was doing something out of the norm by providing her with an opportunity to learn. She was conscious of the fact that she was lucky to be in this fortunate position when many women her age did not have the same opportunities to gain any form of education. Running a surgery to treat the poor was never going to make Dr Rayner a vast fortune, but he obviously considered the education of his daughters to be a top priority and just as important as that of his sons. I like to think that Dr Rayner saw the spark of wisdom and intelligence in Edith, which then convinced him that it would be money well spent to send her to school. It was definitely a radical decision to send the daughters of the family away to boarding school rather than the sons, who were educated at the town's grammar schools, but that was the approach taken by the Rayners, so Edith and her sister Alice remained in fulltime education until they were 18 years of age. Sadly, that is where their formal education ended, as a university education was difficult for a woman to achieve. University places were available to women at this time, but only up to a certain point. They were free to attend lectures and sit the examinations to gain honours, but they were not allowed to become a member of a university or claim a degree in their chosen subject in the same way that men could. So, Edith made the decision to end her formal education at the point when she left Penrhos, although I have no doubt that she would have excelled at university if given the chance.

Despite the seriousness regarding her education, Edith still knew how to have fun and was known for having a wickedly fun streak in her. She would often spend her summer holidays in the Lake District with Annie, where they would go swimming naked in the lakes, despite the risk of being seen by passers-by, and they also wore their skirts far shorter than was deemed respectable. Edith left Penrhos College in 1890 and returned to the new family home at Park Terrace in Fulwood, where her father had taken a new surgery on at Fairview. It was a much more respectable part of town, but would have seen a high rise in the family's cost of living. Why the family decided to make the move is unknown, but it may have been down to the decline of the cotton industry in the late-nineteenth century. It will have also offered the doctor a more relaxed and slower pace of life, but he still kept his surgery on Pole Street, should he be needed there.

Edith and her siblings would often join their father on his rounds to see patients. Doing this first opened Edith's eyes to the many inequalities faced by the working-class population. Preston was a town very much split in terms of its social classes, with clog-wearing mill workers heading up Church Street and along New Hall Lane to the factories, when only a bit further down the road the genteel middle classes dressed in their finery, walking along Avenham Boulevard and through the grand Miller Park. The contrast Edith must have experienced in her daily life must have been stark. The inequality must have raised questions for the youngster. Even if she did not see it in the people, she would have seen the differences between the small, pokey red-brick homes to the larger, double-fronted houses with their grand, glossy front doors.

Despite the mill and factory workers being the driving force behind Preston's cotton industry, they suffered both economically and socially. Growing up in the shadow of the mills and accompanying her father on his visits, Edith would have been well aware of the working conditions endured by the common people. Even from a young age she was determined to fight for a better future for them, and despite understanding the differences between the classes and knowing that the conditions were wrong, Edith was a naïve child; she was surprised to find that some of the local children were already at work in the mills and factories and not attending school like she did. She witnessed children her age heading out of home at 6 o'clock in the morning to put in a full day of hard work while she sauntered down Fishergate to school. It must have been an eye opener for her as she could not have failed to note the differences; whether she knew she was privileged or not, she never acted as though she was any better than anyone else. She was a kind and caring young girl, who fully understood that she had more in the way of luxuries than her neighbours.

One Christmas day morning, the family rose to find that Edith, aged 12, had left the house. Worried about where she could be, her father rushed downstairs to launch a search party. However, before he could put a manhunt in to full force, she returned and explained that she had been saving a few pennies from her pocket money each week so she could fill her basket with little treats for the children who had very little. She had decided she would get up at 6 am, even though it meant leaving the warmth and comfort of her bed, to head out on to Church Street and its surrounding lanes to give out small tokens and gifts to the young children on their way to church. When she returned home her basket was empty. Even at this young age, Edith's kindness and the desire to do good shone through; if she had something, she was always happy to share it with those less fortunate than herself, and this trait was to stay with her for the rest of her life. Once her parents had calmed down and got over the shock of waking to find their child missing, they must have been very proud that Christmas day morning.

As she got older and surer of her own confidence, Edith started to push the boundaries of female expectations. In 1888, while on holiday from school at the age of 16, she became the first female to own and ride a lady's bicycle in Preston. The usefulness of having a bike and her own mode of transport was not lost on her, and she had undoubtedly seen the delivery men and boys riding around town on their bicycles and decided she wanted in on that. At this time, no one would bat an eyelid at a man riding a bike, but for a woman to do so was utterly shocking. In fact it was downright improper, and would surely cause a scandal. Edith must have known from the off that this request would cause eyebrows to be raised, but the strong-willed girl asked her father if he would buy her the bicycle, and despite attempts to dissuade her and some severe reservations, he did (he knew better than to try and dissuade his headstrong daughter). It had hard tyres and one gear so would not have been a comfortable or pleasant ride along the cobbled streets of Preston, but Edith was thrilled with her new wheels. The town's residents on the other hand were aghast; they could not believe they were seeing good Dr Rayner's daughter riding down Fishergate in her bloomers, and on a bike of all things! While the older residents were shocked, it was the reaction from Preston's youngsters which proved to be far more direct. The young lads pelted her with rotten vegetables and eggs as she passed, while the young ladies booed and heckled her as she sped along. Even the local vicar had something to say about it, taking umbrage at seeing one of his star pupils from Bible class pass on her new mode of transport. He had ear marked her as a future teacher for the Sunday school, but he could not get over the fact she had lowered herself to such a debased manner, so that idea was out the window. Quite clearly, none of this bothered Edith. She did not give up her wheels and the resilience shown here would stand her in good stead for her future. In fact, at the age of 18, she decided to cycle to her friend Annie's house in Leicester and cycle back home the next day, a distance of approximately 200 miles. Again, her father tried his best to dissuade his daughter from undertaking what would be a huge physical feat, but Edith being Edith went anyway.

At the age of 18 Edith returned home from school and the time had come for her to decide on her future. As an educated middle-class woman her options were limited, but she knew she wanted to do good and was aware she could not do this with a full-time job. As her bike riding past proved, she was always open for trying new experiences. So, she opted to get married. With her strikingly good looks and genial personality, it is no surprise she had many admirers knocking on her front door. After many suitors, the lucky man was chosen. He was 35-year-old Dr Charles Samuel Rigby of Preston. He came from a large family and already had an established medical practice in the town and was living on Winckley Square at the time of their marriage. He was very keen on the match and refused to take no for an answer, so shortly before her twenty-first birthday, at noon on 7 September 1893, the happy couple were married in a ceremony at the Methodist Chapel on Lune Street. Charles has been described as being a kind and gentle man with a soft, soothing voice, he had a tolerant and supportive nature which is perhaps a good thing considering his future wife's choice of career. He was to be tested to the full in the years to come, as being married to such a vivacious spirit as Edith was never going to be dull.

The wedding was well attended and the church was described as being full with family, friends and acquaintances of the couple, including the bride's uncle, Rev. C.W. Christien, who officiated the nuptials. The wedding made the local press and as Edith arrived on the arm of her father, who must have been relieved that his daughter was now settled, especially with a man from the same profession as himself, she was described as being resplendent in a gown made of rich ivory satin duchesse, trimmed with mechlin lace with a full court train. The dress had been made by Messrs William Grey & Co. of Fishergate, Preston. Dr Rigby had very kindly made a gift of a diamond and pearl crescent for his new bride, and she was attended by her bridesmaids Miss Alice Rayner (sister) and Dr Rigby's two sisters Miss Rigby and a Miss Mabel Rigby. Once the ceremony was over the couple were announced as Dr Charles and Mrs Edith Rigby, as she was adamant that she was not going to concede her Christian name like many married women did at the time. Why should a woman have to wait until she was a widow to regain her Christian name? So, Edith was to be known as Mrs Edith Rigby. Charles was happy with this demand, and at that point he must have realised she was not going to be a submissive wife, but must have admired her strong will too, and I would like to think, even at this early stage in their relationship, he admired and respected her strength of character and independence of spirit.

The guest list was extensive and included many well-known local figures in the town including Mr and Mrs E.H. Booth, founders of Booths grocery stores which sprang up across the north of England, and they very kindly gifted the newlyweds a pair of china vases. Other gifts included a stag's head with antlers from a Mr John Christian, a gong from a Miss Dewhurst, with Edith's parents gifting their daughter and son-in-law a Beckstein piano and cheque. The wedding reception took place at the Rayner family home in Fulwood, after which Dr and Mrs Rigby departed Preston for Paris via London for their honeymoon. Shortly after their return they moved into their new home together at 28 Winckley Square, the grand Georgian square where the town's doctors and lawyers tended to live, and an area that was considered to be one of the most upmarket and exclusive residential areas in the town.

Despite her new-found wealth and status living in Preston's most exclusive neighbourhood, Edith was only ever one small step from causing outrage; having to adapt to a whole new way of life, both as a wife and as lady of the house, was never going to be easy. Her views on equality meant her household was not going to follow the strict hierarchical format of those of her neighbours. The servants were treated respectably and fairly, and were to be considered as members of the family. They were not required to wear a uniform and were invited to dine in the main dining room along with the rest of the family and their guests. It is fair to say a woman like Edith was never going to be the kind of person who would join the ranks of ladies making daily calls on her neighbours to take tea. The drawing room was not her natural habitat, but I do not think anything could have prepared Winckley Square for the force that was Edith Rigby. She was different, but to the other residents that was not necessarily a good thing. The household chores were not something to be palmed off on to the servants and it was important to Edith that she herself was seen to be taking on her fair share of the tasks. One morning, passers-by were shocked and dismayed to see her on her hands and knees scrubbing her own front doorstep. If you were to go to any part of Preston's working-class areas you would have seen many of the housewives there doing the exact same thing, using a donkey stone and continuously scrubbing to ensure the front doorstep and pavement directly in front was kept clean and respectable. It is possible Edith saw the housewives of Pole Street doing this, but it was a time-consuming task that was hard on the arms, knees and back and was certainly not done by the wife of a doctor who had her own set of servants who could do it for her.

Fashion was not a high priority on Edith's agenda and she would often raise eyebrows when it came to her clothes. She was a woman who wore flat shoes for comfort and refused to wear long, restrictive corseted dresses that were accepted as the norm among her equals. Instead she often opted for trousers, which were essential for riding her bike, or loose-fitting pinafore dresses that offered her comfort. She was far too busy to be bogged down with making sure her clothes met with the current social guidelines and would not allow her clothes slow her down, so comfort was the name of the game.

Her ability to be bold and spark outrage paid dividends for Edith when the suffragette cause took off, but things were starting to get too much for her neighbours and she was very much vilified. At one point she was confronted by a select group, who advised her that if she did not change her ways it would be best if she left the neighbourhood as they could no longer tolerate her uncouth behaviour. They did not stop there, and even went as far as accusing her of bringing the area down to slum level. They cruelly criticised every aspect of her life, from the way she ran her household to the way she dressed, and as for her progressive ideas regarding equality for all, we can only imagine it did not go down very well. These were not the kind of people who would take to change very well, they lived gilded and privileged lives which they thought that people like Edith were trying to change, so they treated her as a threat that needed to be dealt with. But at the end of the day Edith posed no direct threat to any of them, she was simply living her life in the manner that felt right for her and her family. Charles quite clearly had no issues with his wife's thoughts or behaviour, and if he did it was discussed quietly behind closed doors. I am sure Edith took on board any wise words he had to share and then carried on with her life. We do not know how Edith felt after being confronted in this manner, but as strong as she was it must have been upsetting to hear these things said about you. No one likes to be confronted and told they are bad for society for just being themselves, and to know your whole neighbourhood was against you must have been a very isolating feeling. We do not know how she reacted following the outburst, but I doubt she was the kind of person who would fall into a fit of despair and cry on her husband's shoulder for too long. I would expect her to deal with the issue in a more practical manner, and what we do know is that the couple who visited her woke the next morning to find their beautifully glossed front door covered in white wash. Edith never admitted to it, but as we shall see later on, she did seem to get a kick out of vandalism.

For a girl who had spent the majority of her life living in Pole Street, where she did not need to put on airs and graces, it must have been quite a shock to then find herself being scrutinised for everything she did and said, but as the bicycle incident proved, Edith heeded no attention to what people thought of her, the only difference was now she was married and had her husband's reputation to consider. Edith's sweet nature perhaps led her to believe that people ought to be nice and kind regardless of who or what you were, because that is what she had been brought up to think. It is ironic to think that it was the so-called refined people of the middle classes that behaved in a deplorable manner and not the hard-working lower classes that Pole Street housed. Residents in streets like Pole Street were close knit communities, they lived and worked closely together and would socialise in the local pub, always looking out for one another. There would have been a stronger sense of community among people who were cleaning their own doorsteps, and what they were wearing would not have been of any great concern to them; they had greater things to think about, like making sure they had a job and a roof over their heads with food on the table. The 'curtain twitchers' of Winckley Square had no such concerns, and the ladies who sat in their parlour windows scrutinising others really should have behaved in a more charitable way towards Edith, and she could have taught them a few things about being kind. Pole Street definitely provided Edith with an opportunity to see the other side of life, as it offered her first-hand experience of life and its struggles. Her early life provided her with a steady platform from which she could build her arguments for a better life for the poor, but it would be grossly unfair to cast her as a busybody do-gooder from the posh part of town. She had lived among those people for the first eighteen years of her life, she had seen first-hand how they lived, how they were treated and what conditions they worked in, so she felt qualified to have a say. It must have felt like a pressure pot at times living where she did, so she needed a release and that came in the form of a project. Edith took on the leasehold of a small bungalow in the village of Broughton, which sits just north of Preston. Here she could spend her time outdoors, getting her hands dirty growing fruits and vegetables. At times it must have been a lonely life in that big house, and with the doctor on his rounds and the servants engaged in their tasks, Edith could cycle up to the village first thing in the morning and spend all day out in the fresh air. For her this was a little oasis to do as she pleased, she could clean the doorstep without an eyebrow being raised or tut being heard.

The marriage between Charles and Edith appears to have been a happy one from the start. However, for reasons unknown, the couple remained childless for many years. That was to change in 1905 when they decided the time was finally right to add to their family, and they made the decision to adopt a young boy aged approximately 2 years old. They named him Arthur, after their brothers, but he was to be known as

Sandy, an affectionate name he was given due to his ginger hair and pale complexion. According to records, Sandy was born in Brighton, East Sussex in 1903, but how he came to be adopted by the Rigbys is not fully clear, as it was assumed he was adopted from the Harris Orphanage but after searching the records it would appear that is not the case. Whether the record has been misplaced over time we do not know, but the lack of information in local records indicate he was not adopted from one of the main orphanages in Preston. He also appears to have been given the rather peculiar middle name of Sintram. What this means and who gave it to him are a mystery, but it appears on census records and his marriage certificate, so is a name he used regularly. The timing of the adoption also raises questions. On the face of it it does appear an odd time to finally adopt a child, but as she was married just prior to her twenty-first birthday, maybe Edith felt she was too young to start a family straight away. By the time they decided to start their family the couple had been married for over ten years, Edith was 30 and Charles was now 45 years old with a thriving, growing practice to manage, and Edith busy with her charitable works. She was also about to embark on her suffragette career, although at the time she would not have known the suffragette movement would take over her life in the way it did. It would strike some people as not being the best time to start a family. Having a young child at home would surely have taken away some freedom for both parents. Regardless of the reasons surrounding Sandy's adoption, Edith and Charles provided him with a loving and stable home, allowing him to thrive and grow into a shy but dependable young man.

Sandy grew up in and around the house on Winckley Square and became a pupil at Preston Grammar School, which was also on the square. He took a keen interest in astronomy and Edith would often take him to the observatory on Moor Park so they could enjoy stargazing together. Being the eldest of six siblings she was used to having younger children around, and she was quite clearly a hands-on mother as she was often seen playing in the gardens with Sandy. Much to the dismay of her neighbours, she would get on her hands and knees with him and start digging in the mud looking for goodness knows what. She would also have him help her with her household chores, such as scrubbing the front doorstep and washing the windows. Can you imagine the utter consternation when the neighbours found out that she had enlisted her young child into this too? It was bad enough for her to do it alone, but to enlist the help of her child was too much for some to grasp. Sadly, the neighbourhood did not take too kindly to Sandy, his questionable origins as an adopted child did not sit well with their straight-laced attitudes and they would often talk about him and his mother behind their backs. When Edith and Charles finally decided to leave the town for a more rural home life, Sandy went with them, he had plenty of space to run around and play in and he only returned to Preston to work and marry when he was older.

Once Edith was married she devoted much of her time to philanthropic endeavours, and in 1899 she founded St Peter's School on Brook Street. This was an evening social group that offered young girls aged 11 and upwards the opportunity to gain some form of education while they worked in the mills and factories during the day. They met two evenings a week and enjoyed various activities, including needlework, dancing and singing. Younger sister Alice was enlisted to help and she would come in to play the piano and her friends, who had a much better understanding of the finer points of needlework than Edith ever could, were called upon to lend a hand. Knowing that these young women were required to work at the expense of a full-time education encouraged Edith to set up this new scheme, and one of the most important roles of the group, other than the social aspect, was that it catered for their mental health as well their physical wellbeing. In the summer months, she would take them out on to Moor Park to play sports with Edith joining in at all times. She also arranged other summertime excursions for the group to enjoy. This was to be a project that Edith was to remain involved with for many years to come, she was very proud of what the young ladies became and was grateful that she could offer them the opportunity to better themselves.

So, life went on quite comfortably for Edith; she was married, had a young child and charity work to engage herself in, but she was always looking for something to get involved in. She became interested in the divorce laws, which at that time favoured men in that they only had to prove adultery to divorce his wife, whereas if a woman wanted to divorce her husband she had to prove adultery as well as either cruelty, desertion or bigamy. It was bad enough that upon marriage a man took all his wife's money, property and freedom, and if there were any children involved he would automatically have custody of them too, with no questions asked. Like other women up and down the country, Edith abhorred the totality of male supremacy that was present in society, they controlled the church, the government, business and were protected by many more laws than women were. However, as we approached the late-nineteenth century and early-twentieth century, Britain was starting to see the beginnings of a social shift towards better working and living conditions for the poor. Amongst this shift were better opportunities for women, including better working conditions and obtaining the right to vote, and this was the crucial point that fired up women everywhere.

For Edith, she had finally found a cause she could become involved in that had the potential to lead to real radical change across the country. She had wanted to be involved in the fight for a better life for those less fortunate than herself since her school days and that time had finally come. In her later teenage years she found herself being drawn away from the Liberal Party, which her family had long since supported, but whom she felt were not adhering to their true ideals; they were also against giving women the vote. In 1905 she joined the Independent Labour Party, swiftly followed in 1906 when she formed the Women's Labour League in her home town – this was a direct reaction to her first-hand experiences working alongside women – and she even served on the national executive council. Obviously this was not just happening in Preston due to Edith's work, this was happening in many towns right across the country. Each town had groups of women who were sick of being classed as second-class citizens, sick of being talked down to or talked over and sick of being ignored. The anticipation of change was causing growing excitement among women after years and years of failed attempts to bring the government to the point of agreement. Now, they finally felt it was within their grasp. This feeling only intensified further when the Pankhurst family, led by Emmeline and her daughters Christabel and Sylvia, from Manchester, created the Woman's Social and Political Union (WSPU). After years of being ignored there was now a platform that enabled working-class women to stand up and have their say, and at last their voices were being heard and they were going to make sure their message carried all the way to London and the heart of government. In solidarity to the cause, and in order to join the fight for 'Votes for Women', Edith joined the WSPU and would later form the Preston branch, but that was going to take some serious campaigning and persuasion as it was not a message all women wanted to hear. If anyone could persuade them it was definitely going to be Edith Rigby; she was going to become an integral part of the fight and she was going to do whatever it took to ensure the message was heard.

Chapter Three

Helping the Women of Preston

Edith was a champion of working women's causes and as many members of the WSPU came from working-class northern backgrounds, she was always going to be a good fit. Unsurprisingly, the more refined ladies of Preston who thought that women deserved the vote decided to place their allegiance with the NUWSS and take a much more dignified stance rather than join the militant cause with Edith. Edith had many gripes with the local mill and factory owners on the grounds of their working conditions, but she had to pick her fights carefully. She did not have the capacity to help everyone so it was important to pick the fights in which most people would benefit.

One of her many campaigns came against W.H. & J. Woods Ltd., a local tobacco manufacturer who forced their staff to work in conditions that were questionable to say the least. Edith had received reports that the building, which still stands on the corner of Avenham Street and Church Street, was not fit for purpose and it had been reported the women working there had to endure abhorrent conditions. After extensive research Edith discovered the women were working in dank, dark rooms that were badly ventilated, causing many of the workers to suffer from nicotine poisoning and sight problems. If that was not bad enough, the women had been told they were expected to work for an extra hour per day with no extra pay – it was at this point the women turned to Edith for help, and this was not something she was going to stand by and let happen without a fight. Appalled at what she had heard, Edith decided she needed a plan of attack and as everyone knows, the best way to get a large company to amend its polices is to threaten its profits, and that is exactly the route she took. She petitioned one of Woods's best customers, The Co-Operative Wholesale Company, to consider their dealings with the company. She helpfully enlightened them to the working conditions in the factory and the proposed changes to the women's working patterns, and urged them to cease trading with the company until conditions improved. Luckily for

Edith they agreed, and before long W.H. & J. Woods had implemented the necessary changes, installed a sky light and introduced a mid-morning tea break for all workers. Edith was fast gaining a name for herself, and on the back of this and other successful campaigns she formed the Preston branch of the Women's Labour League (WLL) in 1906 and became an executive of the league nationwide. The WLL was a pressure organisation set up to fight specifically for the rights of working women, it offered them political representation should a need arise to bring action against an employer. The WLL disbanded after the vote was won in 1918.

Edith was the kind of person who would fight a battle for anyone on any grounds, as long as they were justified, and it was not just campaigns against the larger organisations that Edith was involved in, she also took a personal interest in individual cases that she was made aware of. Often, at her own expense, she would help domestically abused women leave their violent husbands and find shelter for her and her children, and for the children to obtain suitable work. She would also help the elderly and infirm in any way she could. For one elderly local lady who could no longer work and support herself properly, Edith stepped in to secure a new residence for her and even paid her rent until the woman passed away. No one made Edith take on these charitable acts, she simply thought she owed those less fortunate than herself a chance to either have a better life or a dignified end to life. Unfortunately for the good-natured Edith, many people mistook her kind gestures for being nosey and interfering. But, she had been called worse and would never correct these short-sighted people, as she knew how much her help was appreciated by those who needed it the most. She never concerned herself with what the richer members of the town thought of her. By doing her good deeds, she only highlighted their shortcomings. It is sad to think that there were people who poured scorn on those who wanted to help those less fortunate than themselves, but sadly this was the case; many of the rich did not want the poor to get richer as that could throw off the entire social structure. They also did not see that it was down to them to make amends for the poor situations people found themselves in. Thankfully, there were people like Edith who could see beyond social etiquette, she recognised her privileged position and was only too happy to offer aid to those she could. It is a shame her Winckley Square neighbours did not think along those same lines. With their support Edith could have made even more of a positive impact on the lives of Preston's poor. It is quite obvious

33

that Edith had a very strong conviction in her causes and she must have remained incredibly strong to continue in this vain. She was a wealthy woman living in the most exclusive part of town but she never allowed herself to get sucked into their way of living and never expressed any of their behaviour. Despite what must have been painful slights and name calling, she remained resolute and determined, and with the support of Charles she continued on regardless.

One of the biggest projects that Edith was ever involved in at home was her decision to set up a night school for the hard-working girls and young women of Preston, and by doing so she hoped it would provide them with the much-needed release from the drudgery of day-to-day toil in the mills and factories. These girls had been working full time from as young as 12 years old. Their working day would start at 6 am and run until 5.30 pm, five days a week. On a Saturday, they would work a further six hours in the morning. The wages they earned were often passed straight to their mother for their keep for that week. In those days every penny you earnt went towards the upkeep of the family, if they were lucky they might get a small amount back as pocket money, the club cost twopence to attend and I am sure many thought it was worth it. As many of these women would have been working from a very young age to help bring in additional income for their families, they would have had to sacrifice the very limited education they were offered, if any at all. Thinking on this, Edith came up with a way that she could help and she saw the establishment of the school as an opportunity to expand on any learning they already had. She understood how lucky she and her siblings had been in getting a full education. Edith and Alice were lucky to have a father who felt that educating girls was important at a time when not many men thought it was, and she wanted to offer these women some degree of learning. She acknowledged that having an education, no matter how small that may be, was always going to be beneficial for the future. It was decided that the group would meet two evenings a week on the first floor of St Peter's School on Brook Street. Brook Street was an impoverished area of town that had grown up around and in line with the success of the mills. Edith personally rented and paid for the rooms herself and the initial take up was good, with over twenty girls attending the early classes.

Over time their numbers grew to double that amount as word got around about the fun and educational delights that were on offer.

The activities were plentiful and Edith put in a lot of effort to come up with a wide and varied curriculum that would keep the girls engaged and entertained. The club was open to anyone of any creed, there was to be no discrimination on any level, and Edith would not stand for any form of bullying within the group. There were many practical subjects included on the curriculum, including hygiene and needlework, but Edith realised that in order to keep the girls actively engaged she needed to make sure they had fun too, and this was considered as important as a formal education. These women desperately needed an outlet, so Alice was coerced in to helping by playing the piano and they were all able to take part in singing and dancing. With the combined lesson plan, Edith offered the women a place to relax and unwind, as well as providing them with much-needed mental stimulation after a long, hard day's work.

The lessons were not just confined to the classroom either; in the summer months the class would congregate on Moor Park for a game of cricket. In the shadow of the famous Deepdale Stadium, the young women from Brook Street would kick off their clogs and enjoy the warmth of the evening sun while enjoying the freedom to have fun with their friends. The sisterly solidarity formed among the girls is reminiscent of the same bond that the suffragettes would rely on during the tough militant times. As well as games in the park, Edith came up with other summertime activities for the girls to enjoy. Notoriously persuasive, she managed to convince the owners of the local handsome houses in Penwortham and Broughton, to name but a few, to give over their fine gardens for an afternoon so they could enjoy refined garden parties. They would march as a group, all wearing their clogs and shawls; out of town, it would certainly have made for a noisy arrival. Once there, Edith would organise games and activities for the women to enjoy, but unfortunately the stigma of who they were and where they were from was never too far away and they were forbidden to enter the house, even to use the facilities, so other arrangements were made. In an attempt to bring a bit more refinery to the group, Edith tried her best to encourage the girls to engage in more intellectual discussions, she even set up a debating group in which they could discuss the relevant topics of the day. It was important that the girls understood what was going on outside the confines of their own town, with such a monotonous life it was difficult to understand the wider picture in terms of politics and other issues across the country, and being working-class girls they would not have been encouraged to discuss such things at home. To their families it would not have been necessary for them to know the news, but Edith appreciated that if they did it would give them a better well-rounded view on life and provide them with opportunities to engage in discussions with each other. While some were keen to get involved, others sat back quietly and listened to discussions rather than take part, but that is not to say they did not take on board what was being discussed. Edith never forced the girls to do things they did not feel comfortable with, as a group they tried a number of activities but if it did not fit well with everyone then they did not approach it again the future. This club was all about having that much-needed release from the stresses and concerns of their daily lives, it was a pressure valve that released them from their worries and concerns and just let them be free of work and family life for a few hours a week. Their lives were hard and they needed to let off steam, Edith gave them this opportunity and the girls were grateful for that, some of the friendships formed at these meetings were to last a lifetime.

Edith's desire to help improve the lot of the poorer members of the local society did not just stop with the mill workers, she also took a keen interest in those who were in service in the local grand houses. She discovered that they had no social interaction with the family and were forbidden to loiter above stairs. Instead, they were either in the kitchen preparing the family's meals or in the cramped attic quarters where they were expected to sleep and take their leisure time, if they were not out of the house. This kind of treatment would not do in the Rigby household. Their servants were never required to wear a uniform or livery and were permitted to eat with the family at the main dining room table. While Edith encouraged this more relaxed attitude, it did have an adverse effect and caused the staff to be less diligent in their chores, leading Dr Rigby to complain that he often had to fend for himself. Charles was a tolerant, supportive and loving husband, however, not having an evening meal on the table after a long day tending to the sick rankled him and he made sure Edith was fully aware of his displeasure. He very subtly reminded her that it was him who provided everything and that she contributed nothing financially to the running of the household, therefore was it too much to ask to have a hot meal on the table at the end of the day? Edith was not the type of woman to take that insult lying down and decided to teach her long-suffering husband a lesson. She calmly left the house and boarded a train to London, once there she entered herself into the service of an aristocratic family. Unfortunately, she did not enlighten poor Dr Rigby of her plans, and when she did not turn up at the homes of family or friends after two weeks, he decided enough was enough and made attempts to track her down. The fact that he waited a whole week before taking any action suggests this was not out of character for Edith and that he was used to his wife's erratic behaviour. As time went on, however, he became increasingly concerned that she had left him for good. So, he hired two private detectives to hunt her down. What they did not know at the time, and what made their task even more difficult, was that she was working under the pseudonym of Polly Sharples, her mother's maiden name. Somehow, they did manage to catch up with her and when Dr Rigby went to the given address to bring her home, she turned him away advising that her employer did not appreciate his staff taking male callers. With an angry Charles now back in Preston sat waiting for his wife's return, Edith continued with her experiment. Her role as housemaid did not last much longer as her employer soon cottoned on to the fact that his new housemaid was rather dignified and graceful, and when she started translating his foreign correspondence, he realised she was perhaps not what she said she was. On her return to Preston she explained to her husband that she had been well treated and that the aristocracy were not all that bad when it came to their treatment of their staff. It was quite clear that Edith was never going to be the domesticated housewife that society expected of her, but was someone who needed to be free to come and go as she pleased. She could not and would not be tied by her apron strings to the household chores. So, in order to keep the domestic peace intact, a compromise was reached, and the Rigbys hired a Miss Tucker as housekeeper; Dr Rigby's meals were now on time and Edith could continue her good work knowing her husband was well fed.

It is fair to say that Edith's level of research was always very comprehensive, whether she was investigating the working conditions of the cotton mills of Lancashire or within the domestic sphere, she now had a pretty good idea as to what women really needed so that they could improve their current situation. It is clear to see that in the years leading up to the suffrage movement, Edith was undertaking her own evaluation of women's lives, she appears to have had a clear brief in her mind of what she wanted to achieve from all her research across all levels, and as the suffrage movement began to expand she finally saw an opportunity to make a difference but on a much grander scale, and she headed straight to the home of Emmeline Pankhurst in Manchester.

The Pankhurst family had lived at 62 Nelson Street, a modest terraced house, since 1898 and it was here on 10 October 1903 that Emmeline and her eldest daughter Christabel founded the Women's Social and Political Union (WSPU) and where the first meeting of this new organisation was held. The family had been prominent activists in the fight for better social conditions and had fought tirelessly for better conditions for women. The WSPU was an independent women's movement created because Emmeline Pankhurst increasingly felt that the Independent Labour Party (ILP), of which she was a member, was not representing women as well as they ought to be doing. So, after much consideration it was decided that the women would fight their own battles. After all, who would be better at promoting the rights of women but themselves? Women from the ILP were encouraged to join the Pankhurst's newly-formed organisation, and as long as they had no party affiliation, they were free to join. It was important the WSPU remained free from any political alliances and from that moment on the fight to obtain votes for women truly began. Finally, here was a group of organised women who were not frightened to pose difficult questions for the government to answer. Being polite was not the top of the WSPU's agenda, they had questions they wanted answered and they were not willing to sit around waiting for the postman to deliver them news as the NUWSS did. They had to gain support for their cause with the current serving MPs, so the Pankhurst women and others went to the lobby in the Houses of Parliament in an attempt to gain support from those who had shown sympathies to the enfranchisement for women in the past. What they needed was for one of those men to be willing to give over his slot to the discussion of the Women's Suffrage Bill.

It was certainly an uphill battle, but in 1905 the Liberal MP for St Albans, John Bamford Slack, was finally convinced to include a women's suffrage bill. He probably relented because his wife was a suffragist but it did not matter, they finally achieved their first goal. In great anticipation, approximately 400 suffragettes marched on the Houses of Parliament to hear the outcome of the bill. They had managed to infiltrate the building and surrounding areas – some even manged to get into the lobby – but they were to be bitterly disappointed to find that after an eight-year wait, the bill had been talked out. In other words, the members of the House found something else to discuss during that sitting, and did not have time to talk about this particular bill. Was this a deliberate act by the MPs against the suffragette's cause, or was there simply more pressing business to attend to? As it turned out it was a debate involving carts that travelled on a public road at night, and whether they must carry a light at the rear of their vehicle as well as at the front. This was quite clearly a much more pressing issue for the politicians than the liberation of half of the population. The suffragettes may have been defeated but they were not going to take this latest setback lying down. The women gathered outside the Houses of Parliament and passionate speeches were given, and Emmeline Pankhurst made it clear that from that point on the WSPU would attack any political party that was in government which refused to support, or even discuss the possibility of, women getting the vote.

With the WSPU's campaign growing fast, Edith was starting to spend an increasing amount of time away from home as she attended meetings and rallies and got more involved with the WSPU and its cause. The new friendships she was building with like-minded women meant she could become more resilient to the treatment she was receiving in her home town, as the ladies of Winckley Square cast her out even more into the wilderness once they had learnt of her suffragette links. Whether Edith had tried to recruit any of them we do not know, but it is unlikely. People would cross the street when they saw her approaching in order to avoid her, she was spat at and her home was the target of vandals. Edith was stubborn and did little to ingratiate herself with her neighbours, she knew she was not one of them; she may have had comparable wealth and a large house on the square, but deep down Edith was someone who wanted to do good, she wanted to build a world that was fair and equal for everyone, especially women, and she knew these people would not understand that. She unwittingly continued to cause outrage and things became more and more hostile when she was accused of bringing the reputation of the neighbourhood into the gutter, and the residents advised Edith that it would be best if she left the square for good. None of this was really of any concern for Edith as in her heart she knew the things she did were good, honest and true, and what she was fighting for was a just and admirable cause. She never set out to purposely cause outrage or upset and nothing would have pleased her more than if her neighbours had joined her in the cause, but the women of Winckley

Square led affluent and privileged lives and they did not want women like Edith Rigby coming along a smashing that to pieces.

These women didn't want the vote as it meant change, and as far as they were concerned a change like this was a bad thing. They were frightened they would lose their gilded lifestyle, and that more would have been expected of them in order to justify having the vote. These women did not work or pay taxes in that sense, so were they entitled to have the vote? Of course they were, they were law-abiding citizens living in an increasingly democratic country, and no one should be denied the right to have a say on how the country they live in and contributed to should be governed. There may have been a fair amount of distrust among certain people of society, and there were people who were dead set against the suffragettes and their cause. This group was called the Anti-Suffrage League and here is their manifesto stating exactly why women having the vote would be so detrimental to the country as a whole:

(a) Because the spheres of men and women, owing to natural causes, are essentially different, and therefore their share in the public management of the State should be different.

(b) Because the complex modern State depends for its very existence on navel and military power, diplomacy, finance, and the great mining, constructive, shipping and transport industries, in none of which can women take any practical part. Yet it is upon these matters, and the vast interests involved in them, that the work of Parliament largely turns.

(c) Because by the concession of the local government vote and the admission of women to County and Borough Councils, the nation has opened a wide sphere of public work and influence to women, which is within their powers. To make proper use of it, however, will tax all the energies that women have to spare, apart from the care of the home and the development of the individual life.

(d) Because the influence of women in social causes will be diminished rather than increased by the possession of the Parliamentary vote. As present they stand, in matters of social reform, apart from and beyond party politics, and are listened to accordingly. The legitimate influence on women in politics – in all classes, rich and poor – will always be in proportion to their education and common sense. But the deciding power of the Parliamentary vote should be left to men, whose physical force is ultimately responsible for the conduct of the State.

(e) Because all the reforms which are put forward as reasons for the vote can be obtained by other means than the vote, as is proved by the general history of the laws relating to women and children during the past century. The channels of public option are always freely open to women. Moreover, the services which women can with advantage render to the nation in the field of social and educational reform, and in the investigation of social problems, have been recognised by Parliament. Women have been included in Royal Commissions, and admitted to a share in local government. The true path of progress seems to lie in farther development along these lines. Representative for women, for instance, might be brought onto closer consultative relation with Government departments, in matters where the special interests of women are concerned.

(f) Because any measure for the enfranchisement of women must either (1) concede the vote to women on the same terms as men and thereby in practice involve an unjust and invidious limitation: or (2) by giving the vote to wives of voters tend to the introduction of political differences into domestic life: or (3) by the adoption of adult suffrage, which seems to inevitable result of admitting the principle, place the female vote in an overpowering majority.

Because, finally, the danger which might arise from the concession of women-suffrage, in the case of a State burdened with such complex and far-reaching responsibilities as England, is out of all proportion to the risk run by those smaller communities which have adopted it. The admission to full political power of a number of voters debarred by nature and circumstances from the average political knowledge and experience open to men, would weaken the central governing forces of the State, and be fraught with peril to the country.

Alongside this manifesto were a plethora of propaganda, from posters of babies crying because mummy is away campaigning with the suffragettes, to handbills being printed that call upon the 'Men of England' to be aware that their lives, and the lives of their families, are in grave danger and that they must prepare themselves to prevent it. How they thought women having the vote could put people in grave danger is baffling, they appear to have been as uneducated on politics as they accused women of being. The National League for Opposing Woman Suffrage clearly felt the government should seek the approval of all men before granting women the vote. It is quite comical to read further in the handbill that there were 1,300,000 more women than men in the country, so if they were given the vote they would be a dominant political force, and men could not allow that, could they? It would not do for they would become the 'laughing stock of the world'.

The desperation of this handbill is quite shocking for us to read now, but at the time they were deadly serious. They were so worried about what would happen if women got the vote that they launched their own campaign to stop it from happening. What is quite difficult to comprehend with regards to the anti-suffrage campaign is that a lot of the members of these organisations were in fact women, and looking back at this through twenty-first-century eyes makes our understanding of their feelings quite incomprehensible. However, these were very different times and we must pay heed to that and remember that the roles of men and women were clearly defined in society; each knew their place and what was expected of them. So, from the perspective of the women in Winckley Square, their neighbour was fighting to alter their lives and blur the lines of normality, which for some women could have left them feeling vulnerable and exposed. Many women liked knowing exactly what was expected from them, they had been trained from a very young age for what their role in life would be, and here were a group of people threatening to turn that on its head.

Chapter Four

Rise Up, Women!

In the beginning the aim of the WSPU rallies was to cause violence and disruption in the hope that it would lead to widespread arrests of the women, which would in turn lead to a trial and the opportunity to stand before a judge and have their say in their own words. Naturally, all trials are given column inches and therefore provided the perfect platform the WSPU needed for exposure. On 13 February 1907, Edith travelled from Preston by train to London to take part in the WSPU's first ever 'Women's Parliament' at Caxton Hall, near Westminster. This was to be held every year at the start of each new parliamentary session. There was hope among the women that the day before, when the king opened Parliament, that mention would be given to the issue of women's suffrage. Unfortunately it contained no mention of the movement or the possibility of it being debated in Parliament, so Emmeline Pankhurst gave a rousing speech in which she urged the women to 'Rise Up!' which they did, immediately. Annie Kenney was infuriated by the omission and claimed:

> This meeting expresses its profound indignation at the omission from the King's Speech of any declaration that the Government intends to enfranchise the women of the country during the present session of Parliament, and all upon the House of Commons to insist that precedence shall be given to a measure to remove from women the degrading disability of sex.

If the government failed to do this, Annie threatened to bring down the mill workers from the north, of which there were many, to march on Westminster and make their feelings on the matter truly known.

Following a round of morale-boosting speeches, a plan was made that the women would now walk in a planned procession to the Houses of Parliament to hand over their petition in person to the Liberal Prime

Minister, Henry Campbell-Bannerman. There were to be further speeches given and banners raised in an act that proved their motto of 'Deeds not Words' was one they were going to live by. The women were led by Charlotte Despard, a seasoned campaigner who was not put off by the police presence surrounding the area. They were refused entry to Westminster and a scuffle broke out, with many of them smashing windows and chaining themselves to railings. Edith was one of those chosen by Sylvia and Christabel Pankhurst to take part in the small group trying to gain entry to the Houses of Parliament, while many of the others followed close behind. Some did actually manage to breach the defences and got as far as the lobby before they were picked up by the police and thrown out and arrested. Among those arrested was Edith, who was sent to a local police station where she was to await trial the next day. She was sentenced to two weeks' imprisonment in Holloway after declining to pay her fine. This was Edith's first brush with the law, and when news of her arrest reached home, Dr Rigby felt the need to defend his wife and her actions. The editor of the *Lancashire Daily Post* had stated the prisoners 'would undergo the full rigours of prison discipline'. A proud and passionate husband, Dr Rigby responded on 18 February with the following statement in support of his wife:

> Sir, I believe this to be greater brutality in words than anything that has been done in deed by any suffragist now in prison. Edith Rigby from her childhood has given every ability that she possesses... to help her sister women. For at least ten years... she has given every day and all the day to the tasks of visiting, organising and studying... the causes of distress among her sisters. No one but myself knows the hours she has worked at it with... singleness of purpose [undaunted] by opposition, contempt, loss of friends, or anything else... She has been a teacher at a large Mothers' class at St James's Church, secretary to the Preston Ladies' Health Club, and is now connected... with the Socialist movement in Preston...
>
> She is no criminal, but one who has worked might and main for the betterment of her sisters. She never did a wrong, consciously, to any human being, but she is in prison. She is a woman of education and energy and pursues certain

methods [having] tried every other method without result. She is rewarded by prison.

You, Sir, know her, you know of her works, her self-sacrifice, and you think her well rewarded by prison, and would have it used to its greatest severity. A gentler, truer, better-hearted woman never lived. Because she thinks the mothers of this country ought to have a voice in its management... prison is her reward. The infant mortality today is terrible. Women who bring up children are excluded from any representation in the Government... prison for those who wish things altered.

Are women slaves? Is this a free country? Have women no brains?... when they want a voice – prison, aye, and plenty of it.

On Saturday morning last Edith Rigby left her comfortable home at 5:30am to take part in a procession from Hyde Park. She tramped through the mud and wet... to show her faith in peaceful methods – as did thousands of others.

There was no mention in the King's speech that any notice was taken of them though the government knew all about it. Prison is the place for such women.

I am the husband of Edith Rigby, and so can speak of her... It is the truth... these women you think worthy of stripes are martyrs. Do you, Sir, try to realize what they are giving up for this cause, and I am sure that you will repent and apologize.

This response from Charles is so passionate and supportive of not just his wife, but the suffrage cause as a whole, and he is to be praised for calling out the editor of the newspaper and for forcing the issue in to the public eye. He raises so many valid and sometimes uncomfortable questions, not just for the writer but for the public as a whole. Were they really comfortable with what was happening to these women? Was prison the right place for them to be? He quite clearly thinks not and that the government is treating them far too harshly. The powerful message that this statement gives is that these women need representation, how can laws be made about the welfare of children without prior consultation with their main care providers? Weren't women supposed to be at home looking after the children, so isn't it sensible they be consulted? Of course it is. Being written by one of the town's leading doctors adds a certain gravitas to this message, and by describing Edith's good deeds, Charles' letter pricks the conscience of the reader.

Up until this point, as one of her regular good deeds Edith had for some time been a regular prison visitor to Preston jail, so she was astonished to find a Mr Caulfield as chaplain in Holloway following his very recent transfer from Preston. He was both astonished and disappointed to see Edith behind bars. It was her role as a prison reformer that persuaded Edith to talk openly about her experiences in prison, and she took the opportunity to do so on her release in newspaper reports. Following their release from prison, the fifty-seven women arrested at Westminster were met with a brass band, who were to serenade them as they made their way to the 'welcome breakfast' at Eustace Miles restaurant on Charing Cross Road. Edith had described prison food as: 'Better than I expected and fifty per cent better than in tramp wards.'

But I am sure the fresh bacon and eggs that were served up for brunch were eaten with relish, and the coffee drunk with great satisfaction. Along with the raucous welcome and delicious breakfast, each returning suffragette also received a cheque for fifty-seven pounds, a pound for each prisoner. In attendance at the breakfast were approximately 300 women from all across the country, who had all joined together to celebrate the wonderful sacrifice these women had made to the cause. They sat in raptures as the speeches began, Edith was one of the speakers and she talked of her what her experience had been and how pleased she was to have suffered greatly for the cause:

> Prison is a grimy, serious institution. A new experience for many of us who have never known cold and hunger. It is good for us to experience conditions which are quite beyond many people's social horizon.

She then goes on to say,

> It is well administered but in-humanely ill-directed. I've come out a firmer socialist than when I went in and I feel the burden of womanhood heavily upon me because women

Right: Portrait of Edith Rigby.

Below: 1 Pole Street, the birthplace of Edith Rigby.

Lune Street Chapel, where Charles and Edith Rigby were married.

The interior of Lune Street Chapel today.

Lord Lever's bungalow before the fire.

The ruins of Lord Lever's bungalow.

28 Winckley Square, the marital home of Charles and Edith Rigby.

Commemorative plaque, Winckley Square Gardens.

Edith being arrested.

Woods' Tobacco Factory.

Howick Cross stands at the entrance to Howick Cross Lane, home to Marigold Cottage.

The inscription of Howick Cross, written at a time when the Rigby's were in residence.

Right: The statue of the 14th Earl of Derby, in Miller Park, Preston.

Below: Damage is still visible at the base of the statue.

The Harris Institute, where Edith learnt about botany.

Preston High School for Girls, Winckley Square.

Winckley Square Gardens.

Edith on Llandudno pier with friends.

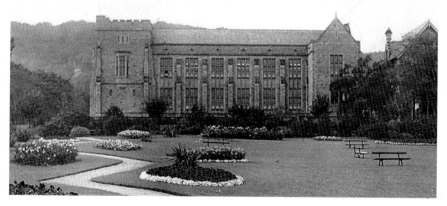

Penrhos College.

Mummy's a Suffragette.

Above left: 'Cat and Mouse' poster, circulated in 1914 by *The Suffragette*.

Above right: 'Mummy's a Suffragette' poster, 1909.

Left: The famous 'Votes for Women' rosette.

A promotional poster.

'Votes for Women' poster.

'God Speed the Plough and the Woman Who Drives it'. A poster encouraging enrolment in the Women's Land Army.

are at the bottom of the scale in a country where they've no share in the government. And all women long to be of more service to the country. God help the Women's Revolution!

The Women's Parliament and subsequent arrests were not all in vain though, as a Mr W.H. Dickinson, Liberal MP for St Pancras North since 1906, decided to put forward the Women's Enfranchisement Bill, which would be debated on 8 March 1907. The campaign had been a success and the time spent in prison worth it. Following her release and before returning home to Preston, Edith stopped off at Reading where she met a young Charlotte Marsh, she was 19 at the time and undertaking training to become a sanitary inspector. Her meeting with Edith clearly left an impression on the young Charlotte, as she went on to join the WSPU in 1909 when her training was complete. Charlotte was to become one of the WSPU's leading stars over the next few years, dressing up as Joan of Arc in full armour and leading processions on a white horse. The imagery of this is striking, imagine how that would have appeared to onlookers and how it would have been viewed in the press the following morning. Charlotte would also be the one to carry the cross at the funeral of Emily Wilding Davison, following her death from injuries sustained from colliding with the king's horse at the Derby on 8 June 1913. It was Edith's strength and courage that had inspired Charlotte to join the WSPU.

It was time for Edith to press home the WSPU's message back in Preston, so, following her imprisonment in London, Annie Kenney came to Preston to help her raise awareness of Dickinson's bill. Annie Kenney was to become one of the WSPU'S most ardent campaigners and foremost leaders. Born in Oldham in 1879 to a working-class family, Annie Kenney was drawn to the suffragette cause after hearing a speech on women's rights given by Christabel Pankhurst and Teresa Billington-Greig at the Oldham Clarion Vocal club in 1905. She was so overwhelmed by what she had heard that it was from that moment on she decided to dedicate her life to the campaign. She began attending regular meetings at the Pankhurst's home and would go on to be imprisoned many times over the coming years, enduring the distress of hunger strikes and travelling as far as America to give lectures and spread the news of women's suffrage. She was to visit Preston and Edith on more than one occasion, and on this particular visit there was to be a WSPU meeting held at the Assembly Rooms, and although shy, Edith gave an impassioned speech:

> I want to tell you plainly that it was not on impulse I took part in the recent suffrage rebellion in London. No one regretted more than I that such methods had to be used. The other women imprisoned with me were of the same mind. There were fifty-seven of us sent to Holloway – they put five of us – I was one – into a cell four yards square. We were there from half past four until half past ten. At least it gave us the only chance we had to talk! My fellow prisoners were not rebels but thoughtful women ready to risk life itself in our just cause. Prison is not a comfortable experience, but you mustn't think we regards ourselves as martyrs, or feel sorry ourselves, indeed for more courage is needed to stand up here before you tonight. Those of you who have spoken at street corners, outside workshop gates and at by-elections, meeting obloquy and derision, are true heroines – not those who have just done seven or fourteen days in prison.

Annie backed up Edith's message by adding her own wit and charm to proceedings and reminding those present:

> The way we're going, we'll see lads of twenty-one making laws for their own mothers!

The speech was well received and the numbers of the Preston branch of the WSPU grew steadily over the next week. With Annie's help and Edith's persuasive manner, a committee was soon formed with Edith taking on the role of secretary, Mrs Alderman as chairman and Miss Ainsworth the treasurer. There were nine other members, of which four would face imprisonment as a result of their involvement with militant action. The meetings were held every Wednesday between 7.30 and 9.30 in the evening, initially in a dentist's waiting room and then above a tea merchants at 41 Glovers Court, possibly Booth's storerooms. The women got to work and soon made this an adequate working space as they cleaned and furnished it with a round table all set for their meetings. The Preston branch of the WSPU was now finally up and running, and ready for action.

Like the Pankhursts before her, Edith used the local Independent Labour Party meetings as a hot bed for recruitment for the WSPU. One of the women she managed to convince to join was Mrs Elizabeth Hesmondhalgh, a cotton winder and wife to a railway signalman. Elizabeth, otherwise known as Beth, was 22 years old and a reluctant recruit. It took the persuasive techniques of her husband, Edith and Annie Kenney to finally cajole Beth into joining, and the friendship she made with Edith was to last a lifetime. Edith would invite members of the branch to her home on Sunday evenings to chat about their own social and personal issues. Wednesday meetings were for business and discussions to do with the cause, whereas on Sundays they met for pleasure and bonding, so all talk of the suffrage movement was banned. Sundays were solely an opportunity for the women to get to know each other and to talk about their lives and families. Edith provided light refreshments and cakes, and she would sit on the floor crossed-legged smoking Turkish cigarettes while she listened to their chatter. Although informal, these meetings had a strict timetable as far as Edith was concerned, for at five past nine in the evening she would promptly get up and declare that it was time for Dr Rigby's suppertime and she had to go. She would leave the ladies to finish their meeting in their own time, but to ensure the door was closed behind them. Quite clearly, the earlier lessons seem to have been learnt in respect of the doctor's eating times. It was an important exercise by Edith to allow these friendships to blossom away from the pressures of the WSPU discussions; the women needed to get to know each other on a personal level and form bonds of trust, as they had to be able to rely on one another if the cause was to be a success. The strong bonds of friendship that were formed upstairs at 28 Winckley Square were to prove invaluable, and some even lasted a lifetime.

1907 saw the founding of the Women's Freedom League (WFL) in London. Unhappy with the dictatorial leadership of the WSPU, seventy-seven members broke away to form their own non-violent, democratic group. They opposed the increasingly violent techniques being used by the WSPU and would opt for more peaceful, yet disruptive, methods such as tax evasion, boycotting the census and peaceful demonstrations. Teresa Billington-Greig was one of the founding members of the WFL. Born in Preston in October 1877, she later moved to Blackburn and Manchester. Teresa had been one of the early members of the WSPU and was influential on the touring lecturing circuit. Like her fellow

Prestonian Edith, she never shied away from any physical action, as one eye witness account describes a run-in with a policeman:

> I did not know it was Miss Billington at the time – nor did I hear what was said but I distinctively saw a policeman hit her in the face when she took a step forward and the lady either pushed or slapped him. I couldn't see which. Then the policeman took her by the throat, she turned purple and it looked as if she was being choked.

Despite the police violence shown towards Teresa, she was arrested for assault and sentenced to two months in Holloway. She was one of the first to be imprisoned for the cause, however her sentence was reduced to one month after Keir Hardie argued that two months was too harsh. In the end, she served no time as a mysterious donor paid her fine and she was released without being put behind bars. Even though she was an ardent supporter of women's rights, over time she become disillusioned with the suffrage movement and along with Charlotte Despard, Edith How-Martyn and others, she co-signed a letter to the Pankhursts advising of their unease and intention to leave the WSPU. They were clearly not alone in their dissatisfaction, and over time there were 60 branches of the WFL across the country, with up to 4,000 members. Their most famous demonstration occurred on 28 October 1908, when three demonstrators – Muriel Matters, Violet Tillard and Helen Fox – unfurled a banner from the Ladies' Gallery in the Houses of Parliament. The women had chained themselves to the grille in front of the gallery, and they were still attached to it when it was removed by the authorities. They had to be taken away to have the locks filed down before they could be released.

The second Women's Parliament was held between 11 and 13 February 1908 at Caxton Hall, and Edith was accompanied to London with Beth Hesmondhalgh, Rose Towler, and Grace Alderman, who had all been selected to take part in an audacious plan to get into the Houses of Parliament. The plan of attack was to include two furniture vans, which were to be collected from a local haulage yard. The women were to bundle into the back of the van and cover themselves with sheets to give the appearance of a removal. Each contained twenty-one suffragettes. The vans were locked and driven along London's bumpy roads towards

Westminster, where they were admitted through the gates at St Stephen's Entrance at precisely 4 pm. The back doors of the vans were then unlocked by the drivers and the women sprang in to action as soon as they could. In one of these vans were the Preston contingent. Edith had been given the task of brandishing the petition and she led her women from the front with Rose Towler in hot pursuit.

The police had been warned to expect an attack by the suffragettes, but they were not expecting it to be in the manner it was. Around 400 officers were on patrol that day and each one was needed to keep the women under control. Inside, Edith urged her women to continue to push forward towards the lobby, but the police were much stronger and came at them in waves and managed to keep them at bay. Edith had her thumbs bent back and her wrists badly sprained in altercations with the police, and many other women were badly injured that day. Soon a policeman's whistle was heard, and the cry came up that they were all to be arrested. All four Preston women were arrested and jailed. For Grace, Rose and Beth this was their first offence, and so they were sentenced to a month in prison at Holloway. Edith did not get off so lightly. She was initially sentenced to a month's imprisonment in the third division. She was separated from her friends and made to wear sack-like clothes – basically she was treated like a full-blown criminal. This was only to last a week as by the second week she joined the second division, where she got to wear a green dress and join her friends. Why she was moved up we do not know, but she served the rest of her sentence there. The others did not fare as well. Grace suffered to the point that she vowed never to go through it again, describing her experience as follows:

> I can never forget the noise of the cell doors banging, all along the ground floor, all along the middle floor (mine) and then all along the top floor – for meals, visits by Matron, Governor, Medical Officer, and the magistrates who were all men in those days. I thought I would go mad.

There was some joy, though, when Edith returned to their ranks:

> Though we weren't allowed to speak, her calmness was reassuring. And we could sneak a few words at exercise time in the yard.

Rose Towler began to get tetchy, she had only prepared enough food for her husband and children to last two weeks. She became so distressed that she was bailed out, and upon her release she fled back to Preston. Edith, Beth and Grace were released shortly after. The three of them lingered in London, taking in an afternoon tea, a play and the 'prisoner's release' lunch. Upon their return to Preston they were greeted with cheers, the mood had quite clearly changed in Preston and Edith later described their time in prison when she wrote to the local paper:

> A year ago, February 1907, three of us from our native town of Preston – unprogressive and self-sufficient Preston – decided to go to prison and thus rouse our town to interest in our movement. Now, in March 1908, we have a large crowded suffrage demonstration to welcome four of us released prisoners.
>
> I am one of thousands of women who are glad to have taken a part in this movement, who have found that they have gained more than they gave – as is ever the case when serving a noble cause in true chivalry.
>
> Could other women know how wonderful it has been to meet local and national workers, to feel the comradeship… which women from the North have given to those from the South, and have received again; which women who have what is idly called 'worldly advantage' have given to others with sadly limited chances, and have received again.
>
> The power of working together for the development of womanhood, and thus of motherhood, and of humanity, revealed through our movement… is not prophetic of the great spiritual strength inherent in our race when women are no longer in subjection?
>
> Do these things not repay one thousandfold for the painful publicity and personal suffering?

It was more than just fighting for the right to vote, it was everything that went along with that, and it was about raising the lot of women as a whole across all aspects of society. But, in order for that to happen they must win the right to vote, and that was the basis of all the campaigns.

On the 8 April 1908, leader of the Liberal Party Herbert Henry Asquith became Prime Minister of the United Kingdom. This was considered a disaster from the suffragette movement's point of view. He was against giving women the vote and put up barrier after barrier in order to stop the Women's Suffrage Bill making it to Parliament. He requested proof that the majority of women actually wanted the vote, but he remained unmoved; even when confronted with the largest rally of the whole campaign he still refused to acknowledge their pleas. Asquith gave the women no choice, the fight had to go on, regardless of what that meant in terms of the level of violence needed. Edith continued to work tirelessly, holding meetings and rallies back home in Preston.

In July 1909 she visited Lytham, where she was interviewed by a local journalist who went by the name of 'Will-o-the-Wisp'. He maintained that he had a strong dislike for all suffragettes, except Edith. She consented to give him an interview and this provides us with a rare glimpse into her thoughts and feelings regarding the suffrage movement:

'What would you have been doing if you had not been engaged in this movement?'

'Possibly playing golf or bridge.'

'It is argued that married women should stick to their homes.'

'That is the ideal. But they don't. Take the ordinary quiet woman, and see the kind of thing she does with her time. Look at what she reads. What does she know, for instance about the care of children in the workhouse. Politically she is quite ignorant.'

'What has prompted this visit to Lytham?'

'Well, we want to influence the people who have leisure – people who have come from the manufacturing towns to live here. We feel they should take their share in the movement. We who live in towns have got it.'

'So that the people who have come here to rest are not to be allowed to rust, as the saying goes?'

'They're not to be allowed to forget that they belong to the places they left behind them.'

'What is the plan of campaign here?'

'It is proposed to form an organization, and carry on propaganda.'

'How, did you become associated with the movement?'

'I happened to be in Liverpool at the time Miss Gawthorpe was addressing open-air meetings at the mill gates, and I sent in my name.'

'So the subject always appealed to you?'

'No. Six years ago I had the usual notion that it was not woman's sphere.'

'You have been to prison?'

'Yes. For a fortnight, two years ago, and a month last February.'

'How did you come to be arrested?'

'Through trying to get into the House of Commons.'

'What were your impressions of prison?'

'Well, I did not find it so disagreeable as I had expected. What really brought me into the movement was this: I was secretary of a Mill Girls' Club in Preston, to provide good education and social classes. I went to the University Settlement in Manchester, and the Warden, a very fine woman, to whom many of us owe so much, put into my hands a book which set up new lines of thought about woman's duties and capabilities. One finds the rest for oneself.'

Edith was a woman of few words, so this interview is invaluable to us in understanding her thoughts on her life as a suffragette. Her answers are short and to the point, and she is quite clearly wanting to get her message across. That message is meant for all, those of all ages and those of all walks of life, whether you are still working or have taken retirement. The success of the Women's Suffrage Bill was to be a nationwide campaign fought on all fronts, and something the WSPU were pinning their hopes on. The campaigning never ceased and Edith drew up a petition that she hoped the rate-paying women of Preston would sign. In order for her to achieve this she spent hours on end walking up and down the streets and knocking on every door, explaining over and over again the reasoning behind the campaign and why it was so important. The petition was then passed to the corporation of Preston, where only five men voted against it. A Dr John Rigg very astutely realised that if they did not accept it then the prospect of militant action in Preston was a very real possibility, and that was certainly not something they wanted on their own doorstep. One of the WSPU's most popular tactics at this time was to harass and badger ministers as they went about their business. Edith was never one to miss an opportunity to work for the cause, and when she discovered the Secretary of War Mr Haldane was travelling from London to Preston, she decided to greet him on the platform of the station and ask if he would give women the vote. She pestered him for answer but he gave none. Not to be undeterred by the failure to pin him down to an answer, Edith turned her attentions to a much bigger target.

On 3 December 1909 Winston Churchill visited Preston to discuss the People's Budget at the public hall. Then aged 35, Churchill was a member of the cabinet in his role as President of the Board of Trade. The People's Budget was the government's policy on social reform, it was the hot topic of the day and the suffragettes were not going to pass up an opportunity to cause disruption. The public hall, when completed in 1824, was Preston's largest meeting space. It was located among the wharfs and warehouses and was the site of the town's produce market, mainly for butter and eggs. The hall served mainly as a site for any large meetings and gatherings that were held in the town, having a maximum capacity of 3,564 people with 1,957 on the ground floor, 807 in the galleries and a further 800 spaces for standing. The main room was a spectacular space with a sprung ballroom and a magnificent organ that had to be shipped by canal barge from Kendal, Cumbria. At a later meeting involving a visit from Winston Churchill, some suffragettes managed to gain entrance to the hall and chained themselves to the seats. The presence of Winston Churchill in the town was an ideal opportunity for Edith and her WSPU members to cause mass disturbance and major plans were put in place to cause as much disruption as possible. Edith must have been abuzz with excitement as she now had an opportunity for her Preston branch to be at the forefront of the campaign, so she had to make sure they were well organised. She suggested that each woman carry a potato in her pocket with a message attached, which could be thrown towards Churchill with the hope that it would either hit him head on, or land near enough for the message to be read. Or, if they were in the process of being arrested, they could lob them through the nearest window – anything to cause disruption.

The police were well aware of the mayhem these women could cause, it was widely reported in the press how these rallies often ended in violence so they had to be ready for trouble. In order to try and keep a lid on any disturbances, all women were banned from attending the meeting, thus making this a battle of all men in authority – including those on the town's council, those in politics and the police force – against womankind alone. Approximately 150 officers were on duty that day and they put up barricades around the hall and its surrounding area with no access to any vehicles or pedestrians who did not hold prior permits from 4 pm. So seriously was the threat of action taken that extra officers were drafted in from London, who ensured that all the windows were boarded up and the glass roof was made secure with a tarpaulin cover. Should a suffragette find herself on the roof there was a hose pipe at hand that could be aimed at her to force her down. Those that lived or worked in the surrounding vicinity were warned that if they were found to be harbouring a suffragette there would be serious repercussions for them to deal with. We do not know for sure if any were caught, but it is quite clear from all these precautions that the police force of Preston was leaving nothing to chance. The night before Churchill arrived, four suffragettes set off armed with propaganda posters depicting a suffragette being held down and forcibly fed. The intention was to plaster Preston with this upsetting image and they were successful in decorating the public hall, Preston prison, the Liberal club and the general post office and pillar boxes.

On the morning of Churchill's visit Edith decided to see if she could gain access to the hall, so she indulged in her passion for dressing up by disguising herself as a shrimp seller who plied her trade in the produce markets adjacent to the hall. She blended in very well and was chatty with the nearby stall holders. Where she got the shrimps from we do not know, but Edith was ever resourceful. Unbelievably her plan worked, and she managed to gain access to one of the smaller rooms adjacent to the main hall in which a smaller meeting was taking place. What she gained from this and whether she got caught we do not know, but I am sure she had fun! Crowds of up to 6,000 started to gather at the public hall and the surrounding streets, and as the crowds built so did the tension. Edith and three fellow suffragettes set off, presumably from Winckley Square, to try and gain access to the hall, but as they headed down Lune Street they hit hostile crowds and were forced back, so they decided to head down the narrow Surgeon's Court passage and on to Fox Street. At about 8 pm they finally managed to gain entrance to the hall, naturally they were denied access by the officials but they refused to leave. The women were subjected to terrible abuse both physically and mentally: they were pelted with horse manure and it got so violent that some of the women were let through to safeguard their own safety. Another group, including Beth Hesmondhalgh, mounted the barriers down Fox Street and started giving their speeches as loud as they could. As soon as she started addressing the all-male crowd she was hauled down by the police, but as soon as she was down Edith was up in her place shouting, 'We are here to stay!' Further police officers were soon called over and Edith followed Beth in to the back of the police van, quickly followed by the others.

Unfortunately, none of the women had managed to deploy their potatoes to full effect and when asked to empty their pockets at the police station the officers were faced with nothing but a table full of vegetables. They were charged with resisting and obstructing the police and it was reported that riots broke out all across Preston that night. It is unsure whether or not Churchill was aware of the commotion outside the hall, but certainly the women had made their presence felt. All four of the women were hauled in front of a judge the following morning and each one given a custodial sentence, with Beth reiterating again that if it raised awareness for the 'Votes for Women' campaign, then imprisonment was worth it – she chose to happily go to prison for one week. Edith was also sentenced to a week's imprisonment, but the very idea of her being in prison in her home town was too much for her family to deal with. Her father, Dr Rayner, paid her five-shilling fine in order to secure her release. *The Times* reported that Dr Rayner got to his feet in the courtroom and shouted:

> This lady is my daughter I will pay my daughters fine. This
> is the third time she has been placed in this position as the
> result of her getting into the hands of hired women, who
> make profitable advertisement out of her.

Arthur, Edith's brother, claimed his sister had been led astray by 'That little painted jezebel.'

He makes this claim in reference to a Mrs Hewitt, who had dared to wear lipstick. The actions of her father and brother sent Edith in to a rare rage and she was beyond angry at their well-intentioned actions. They had gone straight to the police station to pay the fine without discussing this with her first and it caused her untold upset. Edith's reaction was unusual for the calm and placid lady with the soft voice and mild temperament, but they had deprived her of the opportunity to once again highlight the plight of women. I can imagine this caused her embarrassment, especially when her fellow conspirators that night were all happily taken off to prison to serve their week's sentence. Little did they know, however, they were about to face the horrors of force feeding, which was to make poor Beth so ill that she had to be released under the cover of darkness so people couldn't see the state she was in.

Unlike the increasingly pitied Charles, who clearly supported his wife's actions, the Drs Rayner showed little understanding of Edith's cause and also of her character. She was not the kind of woman to be easily led astray: she was an independent, free-thinking woman who had made all her own decisions regarding her actions. It leads us to wonder if they were only concerned of their own reputations rather than Edith's passion to the cause of women's rights, but they had clearly made a huge error in judgement. Her esteemed brother Arthur had become a well-respected doctor in the town, just like his father before him. Like his father, he appears to have been dedicated to his profession and worked up to his death. He was never fully supportive of Edith and her campaigns and thought his sister an eccentric, but it is his daughter, Phoebe Hesketh, who we have to thank for the majority of the stories of Edith's life, as she wrote a memoir of her aunt's eventful history.

If by paying her fine her father and brother had sought to remove Edith from the news headlines, they were very much mistaken. By paying the fine they had only encouraged her to find a way to cause more mayhem and she quickly started to plot her next move. As part of his nationwide progress Churchill headed to Liverpool, so she decided to follow him there on his tour a day later. Witness accounts say they saw Edith mount a chair outside Church Street police station and proceed to give a speech, probably the same one she had prepared for the night before. Once she had finished what she had to say she got down from the chair and threw an object at the window of the police station; when it failed to smash, she punched it and put her fist right through the glass, shattering it to pieces. Luckily for Edith, a policeman had watched the whole episode and she was immediately arrested and charged with wilful damage. She was sent to trial and found guilty – mission accomplished. She finally got what she wanted and was sentenced to fourteen days in Walton jail on the outskirts of the city. Upon her arrival she immediately refused all food and water, and by the fifth day of her sentence she was threatened with the prospect of being force fed. Edith was well aware this was to be the punishment and replied:

> When we are treated as political prisoners hunger-striking will cease. And when we are given the vote there'll be an end to disorderly behaviour.

That was quite a clear message she sent to the authorities, and one that all suffragettes were shouting, unfortunately for them no one was listening and the campaign was about to take on a whole new slant.

Hunger strikes were first used by the suffragettes as a form of protest against the government's refusal to acknowledge them as political prisoners in 1909, for if they had been classed as political prisoners rather than ordinary criminals they would have been treated more favourably in prison. They would have experienced perks such as being able to wear their own clothes, having books to read and food delivered from the outside. They would also have been allowed to mix with fellow prisoners and were exempt from having to do any prison work. It is quite evident as to why the government wanted them treated as criminal prisoners: they wanted to humiliate them. Upon arrival at prison they would have been stripped of their own clothes and forced to bathe, more than likely in front of the other prisoners, they would have to give over their personal belongings and were forced to wear the prison uniform which was often made of cheap coarse material. Once they had been stripped and scrubbed clean in front of the other inmates, they would have to have undergone a medical examination and then put to work within the prison. All this was demeaning and embarrassing for the women, but as so many times throughout the campaigning years the government underestimated their strength and the lengths that these women were willing to go for their cause. It would appear impossible to break their spirits.

The suffragettes argued that their cause was a political one, and it was. They were in direct conflict with the government over its political stance on their right to vote, and it is shocking that they were denied this. Therefore it is right they should have been treated as political prisoners: if they had been, the horrors of hunger strikes and forcible feeding could have been avoided. But, of course, the government could never have agreed to this, as it would have validated their militant actions and made their argument of 'Votes for Women' a legitimate political issue, which they would not concede. They certainly could not be seen to be legitimising the WSPU's cause as it would have been game over for the government if they had. They maintained women were nothing but hysterical and over-emotional beings and they tried their best to break their ranks and spirits in prison, but all they achieved by introducing forcible feeding was to unite the women more and turn public opinion in favour of the campaign. The government was about to make a huge error in judgement by torturing women in to taking food and drink.

The first suffragette to go on hunger strike was Marion Wallace Dunlop in July 1909. She was serving a month-long sentence in Holloway prison after printing an extract of the Bill of Rights and plastering it to the walls of St Stephen's Hall in the House of Commons. She was arrested and convicted of wilful damage. She consciously made the decision to use hunger strike as a political weapon, and was adamant she would only take water despite having an abundance of food offered to her. She claimed:

> I threw a fried fish, four slices of bread, three bananas and a cup of hot milk out of my window.

She also went on to claim:

> They threatened all the time to pump milk through my nostrils, but never did.

She was released after serving three days of her sentence, and even though she had been spared forcible feeding this time, the threat was not an empty one. What she managed to achieve by going on hunger strike was to provide the WSPU with a very powerful weapon which they could use in their fight against the Liberal government. But no one could have anticipated what lay ahead and the torturous and horrific experiences some women were about to endure. There would be many who would not escape as lightly as Wallace Dunlop did, as later that year the government decided to embark on a campaign to start force feeding any suffragette prisoner that refused food.

The government felt they needed to take action, and their stance in the argument was that they had no option but to take this course of action in order to preserve the women's lives. In other words, they were doing them a favour and the women should have been grateful the government took their welfare so seriously. It is a shame they did not consider them worthy enough to give the vote to as well. The issue of force feeding was never going to be a wholly popular suggestion, and it certainly heightened emotions and divided opinion as some backed the government initiative. Surprisingly, some people even made the suggestion the women should be left to starve and thereby be judged as committing suicide, which in the eyes of God and the law was a crime, but the last thing the government wanted was to make martyrs of them. Others were rightly outraged and angry that this course of action was even being considered, let alone implemented. The idea that the government of this great, progressive country would take this action against its own citizens was considered barbaric and an act of torture, surely Britain was better than this.

The actual process of force feeding an adult was a difficult, degrading and painful procedure. After a couple of days refusing food, threats would be made to the inmate and if she continued to refuse all food a male doctor would be summoned to her cell, he would then overpower the often-weakened female in order to involuntarily invade her body. The whole process was likened to the action of rape and left the women feeling shameful and humiliated: the image of the strong male commanding and domineering the weak female is a powerful bit of propaganda that the WSPU were not going to leave unused. The woman would be restrained by up to three or four female prisoner wardens, and would either be held down on the bed or strapped and tied to a chair while a hard rubber tube was forced down through the nasal passage and the back of the throat and into the body. Once satisfied the tube was in far enough, an eggy mixture was then poured down the tube and into the stomach until the jug was empty. The tube was then yanked back up the throat and out of the nose. This procedure was fraught with danger, for if the eggy mixture managed to get in to the lungs it could have had potentially fatal consequences. The indescribable horror and panic, let alone the sheer excruciating pain, caused some women to pass out, to wretch and vomit the mixture back up and struggle to breath at all. Many would gag as the tube was forcibly rammed down the back of the throat, and you could only hope the doctor was gentle. These horrific procedures caused many women to suffer catastrophic injuries to their throats and nasal passages, even causing irreparable damage to major organs, and many still felt the effects several years later. For some it caused complications in old age and contributed to their deaths. This procedure was performed twice a day, with many women experiencing it up to 200 times in total. Edith's own experience of being force fed is described by her niece Phoebe Hesketh in *My Aunt Edith*:

> She had been made to sit on a high-backed wooden chair; then she was wrapped like a mummy in a blanket which enclosed her in the chairback – a far simpler method. After titling the chair backwards, the doctor inserted a tube up her nose while a wardress poured in beef tea.

Mary Leigh, from Birmingham, described it thus:

> The sensation is most painful – the drums of the ear seem to be bursting, a horrible pain in the throat and breast, the tube is pushed down 20 inches.

The press back home in Preston reported on Edith's time in Walton prison and her treatment while there, the *Preston Guardian* reporting in February 1910:

> Mrs Rigby, whose sentence of fourteen days' imprisonment in connection with Mr Churchill's visit to Waterloo expired on Monday 20 December, was released on Saturday the 18th. She fasted for five days, after which she was forcibly fed. She notes that the result is to harden the throat and make the passage of the tube more difficult while the bodily distress is great.

To Charles, the idea of his wife being tortured in this way must have been beyond what he could cope with, but again his loyalty never wavered as he understood how important this was to Edith. She is lucky she was married to a doctor who could nurse her back to full health, as he did time and time again, but how dearly he must have secretly wished Edith would desist in her campaigning, for the sake of her health if nothing else.

The issue of force feeding started to create negative press, which increasingly became a problem for the government. As a result, in April 1913 the Prisoner (Temporary Discharge for Ill Health) Act 1913 was introduced, which quickly became known as the 'Cat and Mouse Act'. The aim of the act was to allow the prisoner to weaken herself enough to be released to her family to regain her strength, at which point she was then rearrested and sent back to prison. This went on until her full sentence had been fully served. However, many of the 'mice', including Edith, managed to evade recapture, only to reappear months later at a rally or meeting. A new plan was now needed to get the women out of prison faster, so Sylvia Pankhurst decided to add thirst strike to her hunger strike, with her mother Emmeline later adding sleep strike. As time went on the government's response became much harsher and various stories started to emerge from up and down the country that the women were now being given sedatives to make them more pliant. Many of them contracted pneumonia as a result of ill health, and some even felt they were losing their minds. With these stories now becoming more widespread, the press and the public started to speak out against the government's actions. Even the doctors employed to perform the task were now beginning to speak out against the barbaric procedure, and soon they started to refuse to undertake such a horrific task, stating that it went against their moral code – they were trained to help their patients, not to make them ill on purpose. Demands were made that the policy be revisited and urgent changes made to the current system. Those who went on hunger strike were later awarded medals by the WSPU, Edith and Beth Hesmondhalgh were awarded their 'For Valour' medals at a ceremony at the Albert Hall in Manchester.

The campaign never ceased and there were protests and rallies up and down the country on a regular basis, but the women devised a new plan of disruption and one which carried a powerful message. It would be one of their most peaceful demonstrations of the whole campaign.

On 2 April 1911, the census was taken in the United Kingdom and the WSPU and other suffragette organisations banded together as they saw this as an ideal opportunity to cause mayhem and disruption. They decided to boycott the count with the slogan 'If we don't count – we are not going to be counted', with approximately 4,000 women nationwide deciding to take part. The census is a government-led programme to obtain a snapshot of the country at a given time, it is aimed at helping to make provisions for the future population, policy making and planning. On the evening of 2 April the householder was to confirm who was resident in his or her home at that particular point, so in true suffragette style they decided not to be at home that night. Many of the wealthier ladies graciously opened their homes to all those willing to boycott the count and they came in their droves, with overnight bags and snacks. This was one big sleepover in the name of women's suffrage.

Edith was one of those not counted and does not appear on any census record for 1911. Charles is listed as being at home at 28 Winckley Square with their son, but there is no sign of Edith. It is not known for certain what Edith did that evening, but she may have travelled to the 'Census Lodge' in Manchester, a large house that had been given over to the women for them to stay in and where they enjoyed a 'census party'. She may have travelled to London to join others on Wimbledon Common, where they feasted on roasted fowl, sweetmeats and tea. She may have even headed to Trafalgar Square, where many suffragettes met to spend the evening walking around Nelson's Column singing and talking. The award for the most daring hiding place must go to Emily Wilding Davison, as she spent the night hidden in a small cupboard in the Chapel of St Mary Undercroft at the House of Commons. Unfortunately, she was discovered by a cleaner and taken to the police station, where she was held for a few hours before being released. Emily actually ended up on the census records twice, as she was recorded by her landlady who took a liberal guess at her location, and by an official at the House of Commons. Being absent from home was just one of the ways you could avoid being counted that night, other ways included spoiling the census form by either filling it in incorrectly or by refusing to give the details of the residents in the house. The chap that called on Grace Alderman and her family was greeted at the door by the two women of the house, but only the men's details had been filled out on the form. When they were advised by the official that they faced a fine of up to five pounds for giving false information, they simply laughed in his face and exclaimed 'We're only females! What d'you want with *our* names?' The man quickly left and no fine was forthcoming. There were many forms that contained statements written by women who claimed that as they had no legal rights in the eyes of the government, why should they partake in this government exercise?

When we think of this boycott, you have to give the women credit as they had a very fair and valid point in abstaining from giving their details to the government officials and the actual act of abstaining from the census was inspired. Many of the reasons given were perfectly understandable, one of the harder-hitting reasons was if they were intelligent enough to fill out an official government form correctly, then surely they are more than capable of putting an 'x' on a ballot paper. Many women simply crossed through the records before handing them back to the official, and while several feared punishments over their failure to comply, no arrests were actually made as a result of the boycott. It was a very clever idea but in the end the census was not ruined by the women's actions as some details did make it on to the final census. But it was not all a lost cause: they still managed to take a stand against the government and cause a few headaches among the officials, and they had a thoroughly good time while doing so!

The numbers supporting the WSPU were continuing to grow, but the threat of prison and the reaction of their families to militant action still put many women off: while they held sympathetic views, it was still just a step too far for some. Other than Charles, Edith's family did not wholly accept her role in the campaign, struggling to understand why she had a desperate need to get involved in such a dangerous and unsavoury institution like the WSPU. Why could she not just be satisfied with the good deeds she could do at home, which did not carry the threat of a prison sentence? But Edith never had any fear of going to prison as she understood the importance of it in order to further the cause, and she accepted her prison stays were not yet at an end, so she retired her post as secretary of the Preston WSPU branch in favour of Miss Bamber, a young teacher from the Winckley Square Convent School. In doing so, Miss Bamber was able to contribute to the cause without fear of imprisonment and the consequences of that, for she would surely have been sacked from her post had she been discovered as an active militant suffragette. Edith fully understood why for some women taking the militant stand was just too risky, but she also appreciated that these women backed their cause and wanted to feel part of the fight and no woman was ever made to feel inferior by Edith, the cause was grateful for any contribution women were willing to make.

We are acutely aware of the militant attacks the WSPU used in its fight, but did some of their acts take things just that step too far? Yes, the cause was a worthy one and one that needed to be fought head on, but can they be justified for the attacks on private and public property, and, worse still, on churches? On 6 May 1913 St Catherine's Church in New Cross, London, was set alight, newspaper reports from the time putting the cost of repairs in the thousands. Some of the church's precious documents were rescued from the vestry, but other parts of the church had become inaccessible so many treasures were lost to the flames. The reporters condemned the attack, which had been largely blamed on the suffragettes. They were vilified for targeting the house of God, and it was questioned if they had any respect or if anything was sacred to them. An attack like this was not going to be popular among the general public and it is difficult to understand why they thought this was a good idea: it would never endear the public to their cause.

Causing disruption was one of the WSPU's most popular forms of attack, whether that was by chaining themselves to railings, smashing shop windows or bringing large crowds to a standstill. On 18 April 1913 two suffragettes by the name of Miss Spark and Mrs Shaw decided to visit the Monument in central London. After entering at the base of the column they barricaded the entrance and made their way up the 311 steps to the top. Once they had scaled the building they locked the security guard in his hut and raised the WSPU flag up the flagpole and unfurled a banner which read 'Death or Victory' over the railings. They then proceeded to launch hundreds of WSPU leaflets over the top down to the huge crowds that had begun to assemble below. The police were called and it took them some time to break down the barricade before they could go up and get the women down. Surprisingly, no charges were brought against either woman.

The same cannot be said when in June 1913 Clara Giveen and Kitty Marion set fire to Hurst Park racecourse. It took six fire brigades in total to bring the fire under control and when they finally put the fire out the damage was there for all to see: the grandstand was gutted as were several nearby buildings. Alongside the wreckage was a placard that read 'Give

Women the Franchise'. Both women were sent to prison, with Kitty going straight on to hunger strike. She was released under the Caty and Mouse Act, but soon found herself back behind bars as upon her release for convalescing she went and put a brick through a window of the Home Office.

Things were to get worse and in December 1913, Rusholme Exhibition Centre in Manchester was set on fire and gutted. Thankfully it was unoccupied at the time (as with all of the WSPU's attacks, reconnaissance trips were always made to ensure there was never any danger to life), and was done to coincide with Asquith's trip to Manchester and the surrounding areas. It was also done in protest at the arrest and imprisonment of Emmeline Pankhurst. Again, WSPU literature was found close by, indicating it was an attack at their hands. Art galleries and museums across Manchester were targeted over that period, with fourteen paintings, including ones by Millais and Holman Hunt, being targeted and destroyed. The WSPU also took a fancy to setting fire to libraries, and in 1914 they set fire and destroyed the Northfield Library: amidst the smouldering remains was a book by Christabel Pankhurst with a note attached that read 'To start your new library'.

The audacity of attacks like these made it evidently clear that the WSPU were willing to attack any establishment they felt were against the campaign, or that represented something that did not fit with their ideals. They set fire to the Orchid House and Tea Pavilion at Kew Gardens, which destroyed the building and many of the plants. But it was not just public buildings that were at risk of being set alight, the homes of prominent politicians were also targeted, including David Lloyd George's home, which they blew up in the hope that the explosion would open his eyes to the plight of women.

They also took their campaigns on to the River Thames and would sail past the Houses of Parliament on boats that had been draped in flags and posters with the WSPU massages. There were many posters plastered all across the city and printed in the newspapers, one of the most popular ones used was the 'What a Woman may be and yet not have the vote', compared to 'What a man may have been and yet not lose the vote'. The poster portrays all the respectful roles women may do such as nursing, motherhood, teaching and factory work and compares it to the male roles of convict, drunkard, lunatic and slave ownership. This poster clearly shows how absurd it was that women did not have the vote and yet those in much less desirable roles did, just because they were men. The government clearly rated the opinion of these types of people over the respectful roles of women. Would it not have been more prudent to base the voting system on those who benefit society in a positive way, rather than gender?

It is difficult to condone the above attacks, which are nothing short of terrorism, but can we say they were wrong in what they did? No members of the public were injured by any suffragette attack, as strict checks ensured all buildings were empty prior to the match being lit and the detonator being pressed. But the cost of repairs and the time spent rebuilding and renovating certainly had an impact on the public. Some had to find another church to worship in, some had leisure activities cancelled and some had to find new libraries to attend. It is easy to see with attacks like this why the public was split when it came to their support of the women, and it is easy to see why some thought the Pankhursts were going too far in their militant stance

Chapter Five

Edith's Last Push

It wasn't until 1913 that Edith decided to re-join the militant campaign. By now she had five convictions to her name, but her most shocking actions were still ahead of her. On Easter Monday she travelled to Manchester with Beth Hesmondhalgh to hear Labour MP for Derby, James Thomas, speak at the Free Trade Hall. They took their seats and listened to his speech, but soon enough Edith had heard all she wanted to hear – she considered his speech to be offensive, so she stood up and began pelting the bemused MP with black puddings. When she had discharged her meaty ammunition she promptly left the hall, much to the amusement of Beth, who later questioned the freshness of the sausages. The ladies left without facing punishment but did leave chaos in their wake. Later, on 11 May, Edith was wrongly accused of tarring the brand-new statue of 14th Lord Derby, the grandfather of the then 17th Earl of Derby, who had been in open opposition to 'Votes for Women' campaign. The Stanley family had long since had links to the town and the statue stood proudly in Miller Park, a grand formal Victorian park not far from the town centre. It was opened in 1867 and is situated on the banks of the River Ribble, it also is only a short walk from Edith's home on Winckley Square so unsurprisingly she was prime suspect number one. Upon discovery of the vandalism, a large crowd gathered at the newly-erected statue as the police and the town's officials were called to witness what was described as an utter senseless act of vandalism. The *Lancashire Daily Post* reported on the crime, stating:

> Someone has spattered the body of the statue with some black viscous fluid resembling diluted tar which has blackened the trunk, arms and legs, and splashed the polished granite base … It was suggested that a syringe had been used by someone not tall enough to spray the head. This fact, coupled with the small footprints in the grass, indicated – not surprisingly – that the culprit was a woman, or, two women.

Outrage poured out of the park and through the streets of Preston, soon crowds of more than a hundred were gathered to see poor Lord Derby decked in tar. The police investigation of the surrounding area yielded only a small success: they found a white handkerchief in a bush. All the evidence, albeit one hanky, surely proved this was done by the hand of a woman. It took great effort to clean the statue, in fact you can still see the remnants of the tar today. A film recorded at the time by Will Onda shows the damage caused and the attempt to clean the statue. Edith vehemently denied having done what the local officials called an 'abhorrent act of vandalism' until years later, when she confessed to having arranged for it to be done. Edith was not a woman to disown her acts of vandalism in the name of women's suffrage, she was a proud suffragette and had previously done much worse than tarring a statue, but this attack was on her doorstep and that may have explained why she did not confess at the time. We do not know that for sure, however, and it may be down to other reasons such as the fact that her husband Charles was a member of the Freemasons and was at the same lodge as the earl's grandson. They were both members of the Stanley of Preston Lodge and I doubt it would have been well received in the lodge if the wife of a fellow mason had admitted to tarnishing the statue of its most important member's grandfather.

The Stanleys had been a prominent family in Preston, with previous earls having represented the town in the Houses of Parliament. If she was the culprit, she perhaps felt she had misjudged the situation and had not expected the anger it created in the town. It was not worth running the risk of upsetting the locals any more than she already had done, and it would have been a shame if she lost the hard-fought support she had worked tirelessly to win in Preston. She may also have felt that Charles did not deserve to be ousted from the Masons due to her wrongdoing, considering the love and loyal support he had given her so far. A fifty-pound reward was offered to anyone who could hand the perpetrator in to the police, which was never claimed, and the statue is still marked today with the remnants of the attack. I personally do not think Edith was directly responsible, she was a clever woman and surely she must have been able to read the local feeling and what effect an attack like that would have. But I do believe her when she says she knew who was behind it and may even have given them some gentle encouragement to carry out the attack. Edith was good at encouraging others to carry out low level attacks when she was unable to, and she managed to persuade a local suffragette to travel to Blackburn to set off explosives inside two cannons in a park before setting off for Ewood Park, home of Blackburn Rovers Football Club, and setting fire to the main stand. Once she had successfully set the blaze she hopped back on the tram towards Preston and headed straight for Fulwood golf course, where they poured acid all over the lush green fairways.

The campaign was now at a crucial stage and for Edith it was time to step it up a notch. The defining and most shocking acts of her whole militant campaign career came about in one week in July 1913. The defeat of Mr Dickinson's Representation of the People Act (by forty-seven votes), and comments made by Labour MP Sir Joseph Compton-Rickett that women in Parliament would prove to be of no benefit to the community, made Edith see red and enough was finally enough. On 5 July, she travelled by train to Liverpool where she headed straight for the Cotton Exchange. After smashing a window to gain access she went straight to the basement where she planted an explosive device. The 'bomb' went off with great noise and smoke, but at no point was there any danger to human life – that was never the intention. If it was, she would have planted it out in the open, perhaps under the foot of the Nelson monument in the square. Edith took full responsibility for the explosion when she handed herself in to the police a few days later, claiming in her statement that:

> I wanted to tell you that I myself did this without any aid. It was my own planning, and it was not authorized.

She went on to claim all she wanted to do was to highlight how easy it was for a woman to get hold of the ingredients to make such an incendiary device. It was certainly a warning shot to the authorities. Newspaper reports from the time reported of a loud explosion which alerted the authorities and when they arrived at the scene they discovered:

> A fractured iron cylinder, a piece of fuse, lead and other materials.

The materials were over a foot long and an inch and a half in diameter. Despite successfully detonating the device and causing significant damage to the infrastructure of the building, Edith did admit to bungling the attack as she failed to attach the necessary WSPU suffragette banners. She later posted these in a nearby post box with the following message:

> To Mr McKenna, London: If Sir William Lever had been as loyal to us and the Liberal Party as Lancashire is being to its King this would not have happened.

With many targets to choose from there was a logical reason as to why Edith opted for the Cotton Exchange, her argument being that the Lancashire cotton industry was built up across the north of England by women's labour, labour that made the mill owners vast fortunes while these women couldn't even vote. She was so angered by the injustice of it that she felt the need to make her message known to the wider public. Edith managed to escape from Liverpool and headed home for Preston, but her latest onslaught was not finished. Unfortunately for Lord Lever, this was not the last time Edith had him on her radar. A few months prior to this event, she had heard reports of lavish parties being held at Lord Lever's bungalow up on Rivington, roughly 14 miles from Preston. The guests were said to include the Prince of Wales and Lloyd George, which peaked her interest even more, so she made a trip to see for herself this bungalow of pleasure. She was astounded to discover a menagerie of animals that were better treated than some of the mill hands in and across Lancashire. Again the injustice of this would have riled Edith up to simmering point and to the point of needing to take action. To Edith this was a show of absolute capitalism, and in her mind it should be destroyed, so that is what she intended to do. This was very much an independent attack and does not appear to have been sanctioned by the WSPU. When she arrived back home she plotted the destruction of the pleasure palace, deciding she would need to get hold of a keg of paraffin, a place to store it safely and also transport to get her and her accelerant safely back to Rivington. In the early hours of 7 July she headed back to Rivington to unleash her inferno. She had enlisted the help of local man Albert Yeadon, who was a member of the local Independent Labour Party (he and his wife had strong leanings towards the suffragette cause and would remain in the Rigby's circle until Edith relocated). Between them they managed to obtain a large amount of paraffin that they then loaded in to the back of Dr Rigby's car, which she borrowed along with the chauffeur. The doctor, the chauffeur and Yeadon, to a certain degree, had no idea what Edith was up to.

Once they arrived at Rivington, Edith dismissed the chauffeur to the local pub to enjoy his sandwiches while she and Albert unloaded the car and carried the paraffin towards the bungalow. When they were close enough Edith dismissed Albert, claiming, 'I must finish this job myself, I can't have you involved any further in our work'. She walked around the property several times, ensuring there was no one home. Sir William and Lady Lever were dining with King George V and Queen Mary at Knowsley Hall as guests of the Earl and Countess of Derby at the time of her planned attack. When she was satisfied it was empty, she set numerous smaller fires in the grounds and smashed a window, pouring paraffin into the property before setting light to a taper. Once alight, the fire took hold quickly. It had been a dry summer and the bungalow was made of wood, so it did not take long for the fire to spread. In fact she utterly destroyed the building until nothing was left except the shell. Edith made a quick retreat back to the waiting car and made her getaway. The *Bolton Journal* reported that the authorities were alerted to the fire at around half past one in the morning, by which point the fire was burning ferociously all around. At half past two, firefighters from Horwich Brigade arrived and attempted to tackle the blaze. It was reported that there was £20,000 worth of damage with many fine paintings and furniture being destroyed. Edith wasn't going to make the same mistake this time as she had done in Liverpool, and ensured she left the suffragette propaganda behind. A message was found which read:

Lancashire's message to the King from the women 'Votes for women due' – Message to the King, Liverpool: Wake up the Government. First give us a reason to be loyal then try us.

On 10 July Edith handed herself in to the police and admitted to the Liverpool explosion and the arson attack at the bungalow at Rivington. The trial was reported in the national press and on 11 July *The Times* reported a speech that Edith gave from the dock, which she hoped would be relayed to the King and Sir William:

I want to ask Sir William Lever whether he thinks his property on Rivington Pike is more valuable as one of his superfluous homes occasionally to be opened to the public, or as a beacon lighted for King and Country, to see that here are some intolerable grievances for women.

These were by far the most serious attacks Edith had ever undertaken in the name of the suffragettes and she was sentenced to nine months hard labour in Walton jail under the cat and mouse regime. Between July and December she was released and rearrested on several occasions. Despite her sentence, she was not forgotten in Preston. She was remembered in church services at the Congregational church when a group of women started to chant 'God save Edith Rigby and all women who are being tortured for conscience sake!' In the town's market square, women continued to hold their rallies and give their speeches, despite being physically and verbally abused. All the while, Dr Rigby was at home in Winckley Square with Sandy missing Edith, and worrying at what horrors she was enduring in prison. Edith's actions caused him great worry and anxiety, but he remained her biggest supporter and never failed to speak out publicly in her defence. He questioned whether the government was right to use torture as the best method to restrain these women. On 11 September 1913, Charles wrote the below letter to the *Lancashire Daily Post* defending his wife and condemning the government's use of force feeding, which he likened to torture, the anger that comes through in his words is clear:

> Sir, The re-arrest of Mrs Edith Rigby for the fourth time, as chronicled by you, must be my excuse for troubling you. She has again gone to prison and hunger-striking like a sheep to the slaughter. And this will have to be repeated at least fifty times if her sentence is to be carried out. Mr McKenna must be greatly pleased at this success – one woman to be fifty times without any food for as many days as the conscience of the medical officer will allow...
>
> Years ago I wrote in your journal that English women were free women... and would not submit to injustice. My words are being borne out by their deeds. They will not tolerate the present conditions. They will have the vote. You may torture them but that does not deter them. You and your party... have brought in this Act of Torture.
>
> I wonder if you are satisfied with women being repeatedly brought to the verge of death, then liberated, afterwards brought back to the same torture? Even their gaolers pity them, but they have no power. It is you and your party who are responsible...

You may say that she is sentenced for an outrage… You are outraging your principle that taxation and representation should go together…

It has been thrown in my teeth that I should have restrained Edith Rigby. How have the powers that be, with all their forces, restrained her? By torture.

I have never met a person who does not believe that some women ought to have the vote… I could wish that the women would go on household strike and let men be placed as I am. I am told the State is but a bigger house; it must be managed on the same principles. Take the wife from the homes, and I know from practical experience how it works; there is chaos… If your wives were taken from your homes for a few weeks you would realize it was time to give them justice. The country needs their help as much as the home needs it. By giving them justice there will be no need for an act such as the 'Cat and Mouse' torture. The energy that has been shown in trying to get the vote will be expended in benefiting the country… a state of unrest is felt on all sides; lawlessness is increasing with new methods. Why? Because you are denying women justice.

When Edith was released on licence, it was home to Winckley Square and Charles that she went. On one occasion when the police came to re-arrest her, Edith decided to take her chances and escape out of the back door, where she hopped on her bike dressed as a workman. Whether she knew at the time where she was going we do not know, but she resurfaced in Ireland where she remained in hiding for several weeks. Little is known about her time in Ireland and it is unclear if Charles even knew her whereabouts, but she must have been aided by a network of suffragettes. He wrote the below letter, which has been reproduced in *My Aunt Edith*, to Edith's old friend Annie. His anguish and concern are clear to see:

Dear Annie,
Thank you very much for your note of sympathy. As you say it is a difficult business to decide, but for me there is only one course and that is to back Edith. I know her perfect sincerity and love of justice; she feels it to be the only course

her conscience allows her to follow, is willing to suffer contumely, blows, loss of friends and kindred starvation and so on to prove her sincerity, and she has suffered, never you fear, to see her as I have – almost a shadow, scarcely able to stand, with the smile of an angel and the courage of a lion, a front as undaunted as any hero that ever lived. Then I should be the veriest villain on earth if I was not willing, and thankful also, to be able to back her with every power I've got. I think her little short of an angel, and I'm sorry I cannot do more to help her. I've to be passive, I must keep the home together, look to the boy, and be able to afford her shelter and help whenever she needs it. I do not have the moral courage to face what she has done; I doubt if I could do it for any cause. It makes me ashamed and I feel so unworthy of her, and I know how many a time I've made it harder for her, because, partly, of seeing it in her light. But I'm perfectly and absolutely sure she is right, and I believe the cause is gaining daily, and before this year is out the vote will be won.

I don't know where she is, we can communicate with each other, but where she is or what she is doing I know not beyond this; she is engaged in a work of great importance, working daily, not engaged in militancy, and she has promised she will not do this without giving me due warning and asking my consent (which I should not withhold). She says she is gaining strength, is happy, would much like to see us, but will be away four, or more, months, but hopes to spend next Christmas with us. This is about all I can tell you.

A cause that has people like her at its back is bound to succeed, and there are many as such, and they will do more yet if necessary…

Edith later resurfaced at a house in Deptford, where she made contact with Christabel Pankhurst and a meeting was quickly planned in Preston at the public hall. Rumours were rife that Edith was about to return and put in appearance at the meeting, and the police were leaving nothing to chance. They ensured the building was surrounded so there was no chance Edith could enter or leave without them knowing about it, but they quite clearly did not know Edith as she walked right passed them in disguise. Indulging in her passion for dressing up, she wore a bright pink feathered hat, and as she climbed the stage to deliver her speech it did not take the audience long to realise Edith had returned. She had been away from home for approximately nine months. As soon as the police realised they had been duped, Edith was promptly arrested and returned to prison to see out her sentence.

On 28 July 1914 the First World War broke out across Europe, and many men were called up to the forces to go and fight on the continent. These numbers included many men from Preston and with a barracks in the town it was a hotbed for recruitment. The decision was made by the Pankhurst women to disband the WSPU in order to give women the opportunity to help with the war effort. Despite good intentions, this did not go down well with all the members - Edith being one of them. In response, in March 1916 Charlotte Marsh launched the Independent Women's Social and Political Union and Edith, along with Dorothy Evans, founded the Preston branch. It was important to Edith that the issue of women's rights did not get lost among the tumult of war. They were determined to keep campaigning, albeit now peacefully and quietly. Despite their best intentions, the IWSPU did not last long and it was disbanded in 1918. Following the disbandment of the WSPU, the Pankhursts founded the Women's Party in 1917, which was to become a minor political party and one that would continue to fight for equal rights for women in the home, the workplace and in society. While it was important to Edith to ensure all the hard work that had already been done did not go to waste, she was well aware that the campaigning could not continue in the way it had. As the young men of the Preston Pals marched through the town to the train station to head off to war, she realised there was now plenty of work to be done here at home to ensure those left behind had plenty to survive on. With the main bread winners now fighting on the battlefields of Europe, it came down to the women to make sure the country still thrived.

Preston's war effort was commendable. It is thought approximately 2,000 men died fighting for their country, but the women left at home ensured they did their bit too. A group of notable local ladies set up a committee to provide a free buffet service to any man in uniform at the train station, for those leaving to go to war or those returning injured. They managed to recruit nearly 700 women who helped at the train station to give out food and drink, working twelve-hour shifts so that the buffet could be open twenty-four hours a day from 1915 to 1919, after which its hours reduced. The Preston Free Buffet was set up in the waiting room on the main central platform, and it gave the war-weary men an opportunity to rest and relax, to read a newspaper or to write a letter home. The free buffet proved to be a welcome and appreciated service, and news of it soon spread with many thank you letters being received each week. It was funded purely from charitable donations and at its peak was serving approximately 3,250 men a day. The logistics of serving all these men is to be admired. By the time the buffet closed it is thought more than 3.25 million had been served by the women of Preston. It is not known if Edith provided any assistance to the service as she was now living out of town, but it is known that some of her fellow Preston suffragettes lent a hand, as did the ladies of Winckley Square.

Now that militant action was over and a new challenge was in their midst, it was time for the women of the United Kingdom to finally show their full worth to the government and to step in to the shoes of those men who had left. The time had finally come where they could desist from campaigning and really show how important women were to the fabric of the country. The idea of women being helpless and emotional beings was gone, and in place of that women became capable, reliable and important. A massive change was on the horizon due to the global industrial nature of the First World War. In a way it was a war of materials, of who could produce the most equipment to sustain an unmoveable front, and women played a major part in that; through need, society changed, classes mixed and women's roles were transformed. Once the war was over everyone struggled to return to their pre-war society-dictated station. Women were now empowered and men, via their experiences in the war, and from factory bosses to injured soldiers being cared for, woke up to the value of women in a heavily changing society, and there was no way women were just going to recede back in to the shadows to resume where they had left. Since the time of the First World War we have gone from horses to air planes, and from low life expectancy to a greater understanding of life-prolonging medicine, and women's contributions to this were just as valuable as men's, but there had to be a certain amount of give and take on both sides of the gender gap in order for change to really happen. As the country emerged from war in 1918 women were finally granted the right to vote, albeit if they met with certain criteria. The franchise was not extended to women on the same terms as men, but this was the biggest progress they had achieved and it was to be celebrated. As for Edith, the next chapter in her life was about to begin as she found her skills for being proactive and her kind, generous nature could be used elsewhere and for the greater good of the country. Rather than fight against the government, it was time to fight with them – the enemy was far greater now than it had ever been.

Chapter Six

Men and the Media

The fight for suffrage in the UK is predominantly thought to have been driven by women, and it is so often assumed that men did not get involved in the campaigns. Men are assumed to have been set against women getting the vote, but it would be remiss of us to dismiss the importance that men played in the years leading to female enfranchisement. Their support for women's suffrage is often overlooked as it has always been considered to be a women's concern, but it would be unfair not to acknowledge the men that did assist the suffragettes in their fight for a better future. Back in 1866, John Stuart Mills MP and Henry Fawcett MP became the first men to publically support female suffrage, by doing this they publically acknowledged there was a need for women to be heard and given the vote. In 1893, the newly formed Independent Labour Party (IPL) realised that the Liberal Party were neglecting the working-class voters so they became chiefly concerned with winning the vote of working-class men, but that did not stop the likes of Keir Hardie and George Lansbury campaigning from within the party on behalf of women.

It was not just politicians who stepped up. Men such as Frederick Pethick-Lawrence provided the financial support that revolutionised the WSPU's approach to campaigning with the introduction of new methods of publicity and propaganda. Then we have the long-suffering husbands of the suffragettes themselves. Some media outlets portrayed them has hen-pecked, left at home holding the baby to fend for themselves while their wives were out on demonstrations and getting arrested. However, were many men who supported their wives and backed them all the way. To be fair, if a woman was going to be a successful suffragette she need the support of her husband. Through twentieth-century eyes the men portrayed in the propaganda posters come across as pathetic and desperate as they seem unable to cope without their wives, whilst we view the supportive husbands as strong and dependable who can keep the household ticking over whilst taking care of the children. It raises the question: did these men bemoaning a life of being a suffragette husband actually exist, or were they the invention of the anti-suffragists in an attempt to raise anger and venom towards women? One fictional man, at least, who fits the description of a hard-done-to husband is Mr Banks in Disney's *Mary Poppins*. He did not back the cause ('you know how the cause infuriates Mr Banks' Mrs Banks claims on her return from a speech by Mrs Pankhurst), and the paraphernalia had to be hurriedly packed away lest he come home and find his wife draped in a 'Votes for Women' sash. What his reaction would be we if he did see it we do not know, but it would have not been too dissimilar from that of many middle-class men of the time. We know that Dr Charles was a pillar of strength for Edith for all of their married life. We read the passionate letters he wrote to the press and to her friends offering her his full support and admiration. This was brave in itself: he did not know what reaction he would have received from the local community and he could have easily been shunned by society just like Edith was, but he backed her all the same.

Were other men as understanding as Charles? Well, we must assume that not all husbands supported their wives, and that some gave them an ultimatum of joining the WSPU or risk their family life. Many women would have been supressed by the men in their lives and would have retreated back into the family fold, too scared to voice their support, but then there must have been some that were strong enough to defy their husband's orders. After all, wasn't that the aim of the fight, to break free from the restrictions men consistently put on women's lives? In order for the suffrage campaign to be successful, women who went out to demonstrate needed the support network and encouragement from the men back at home. They needed to know that when they were at meetings or on demonstrations that their husbands and children were ok.

Emmeline Goulden married Richard Pankhurst in Manchester in 1879. He was a barrister by profession, but also an ardent fighter for free speech and women's rights and fought tirelessly to bring about legislation to improve the lot of women across the country. Both Richard and Emmeline would attend rallies and demonstrations together, including the meeting of the Social Democratic Federation at Trafalgar Square in November 1887. Hordes of supporters marched on London only to find Trafalgar Square blocked to them on their arrival by the police. Violence ensued and many people were injured, but watching on were the Pankhurst couple and as members of the Fabian Society they began to protest against the police brutality they saw that day. Richard was a supporter of women's rights long before he met his future wife. In 1870 he had written the first draft of the Women's Disabilities Removal Bill, which was later read in the House of Commons and made it as far as a second reading, but was to be abandoned on the order of William Gladstone. Not to be put off by this, he later wrote the Married Women's Property Act, which after many revisions was passed in 1882, replacing an earlier act of 1870. Despite the considerable age difference, the marriage between Richard and Emmeline was an ideal love match, they had five children together and lived comfortably in Manchester and London. In normal circumstances Emmeline's life should have focused predominately on the upbringing of her children, meeting the needs of her husband and maintaining a suitable home for the family, but as Emmeline herself explains it was her husband's 'firm belief that society is as well as the family stands in need of women's services', and so Mrs Pankhurst continued her work for the Women's Suffrage Society (WSS) while her children were still young.

During her early married life and through her work with the WSS, Emmeline Pankhurst had seen farm labourers become enfranchised by using violence and militant action and this sewed the seed in her mind for her future involvement in the WSPU. For the time being she returned to public office, and with the support of Richard she built up her knowledge of what life was like in the schools, warehouses and factories and the drudgery of these institutions and the impact that had on the workforce. All this knowledge made her well placed for her future role as suffragette-in-chief, but unfortunately Richard would not live to see his wife and daughters take on the British government in the fight as he sadly passed away in July 1898. His knowledge, support and convictions ensured Emmeline was well prepared for the fight.

Husbands up and down the country were either in fear of their wives getting involved with the WSPU and becoming a suffragette, or they were in favour and actively encouraged them to join. Beth Hesmondhalgh of Preston was actively encouraged by her husband to sign up; when Edith had failed to persuade her, it was down to him to convince his wife it was a just cause that she must join. He was a railway signalman and she was cotton winder at a local mill and they must have known that any form of imprisonment could potentially threaten her job and therefore the family income, but still he supported her and put no barriers in her way. This level of support and encouragement from their husbands must have eased the worries of women like Beth, who left to her own devices may not have joined the campaign as fully as she did. Husbands of the most ardent suffragettes had to be just as strong willed as their wives, once they were in prison it would be down to the men to ensure the children were fed and looked after and the house kept in order. They had to develop a thick skin to deflect the name calling and negativity that being married to one of these women attracted. I like to think the menfolk would communicate with one another when their wives were in London or at some rally: sharing their worries and concerns with each other may have helped them lessen the burden of concern. We know how much Edith suffered at the hands of her neighbours on Winckley Square, so with Charles being a doctor he was putting his very livelihood at risk. Men were supposed to keep their women in check and on a tight rein, they certainly should not be allowing their wives to travel up and down the country attending meetings and rallies that had the potential to turn nasty very quickly.

Obviously not all husbands were supportive, many of them simply banned their wives from attending meetings and from being involved in any way with the movement. These men were firm believers that a woman's place was at home with the children. The women that did defy them were incredibly brave and strong willed and must have agonised over the decisions they made. The biggest fear was a change to order and structure, in their minds they were the supreme beings and expected it to stay that way despite it meaning their wives and daughters were subjugated and supressed. It is quite clear that without the support of their husbands it would be very difficult for any woman to join the cause without making some serious sacrifices, but even if you had managed to convince your husband, fighting for women's suffrage and convincing the politicians was something else entirely.

It was not just from within the marriage that men supported the suffragettes. The Men's League for Women's Suffrage (MLWS) was formed in 1907 and they supported a more ethical and legal approach to campaigning, while the Men's Political Union for Women's Enfranchisement (MPUWE) was formed in 1910 and they supported a much more direct and physical approach, which is detailed in the leaflet below:

OBJECT
To secure for women the parliamentary Vote on the same
terms as it is or may be granted to men.

METHODS
1. Action entirely independent of all political parties.
2. Opposition to whatever Government is in power until
   such time as the franchise is granted.
3. Participation in Parliamentary Elections in opposition
   to the Government Candidate, and independently of all
   other Candidates.
4. Vigorous agitation and the education of the public
   opinion by all the usual methods, such as public meetings,
   demonstrations, debates distribution of literature,
   newspaper correspondence and deputations to public
   representatives.

MEMBERSHIP
Men of all shades of political opinion, who adopt the objects
and the methods of the union, are eligible for Membership.
Minimum Subscription, 1/-. [One shilling]

Each member had to make the pledge and pay the subscription, once
they had they were considered to be a fully-fledged member of the fight
for women's rights. In 1909 the Men's Committee for Justice to Women
(MCJW) was formed and they sent the below petition to the king in the
hope it would rouse support for the cause:

The Humble Petition of the undersigned, being loyal and
dutiful subjects of your Majesty:
Sheweth:-
1. Your Petitioners submit this Petition on behalf of the
   Men's Committee for Justice to Women.
2. For many years past large numbers of Your Majesty's
   subjects, who are women taxpayers and as such share
   with their other fellow citizens the obligations and
   burdens necessary for the maintenance and defence of
   the Realm, have urged that they as a matter of right and

justice, should also have a share in the same way as men citizens of saying how such taxes should be raised and spent, and by what laws and in what manner this Realm should be governed.

3. For this purpose societies of women citizens have been organised to promote the passing into law of the measure which shall confer on women citizens the same political rights as are enjoyed by men. Among such societies are The Women's Social and Political Union and The Women's Freedom League. These two societies alone directly represent in their membership many thousands of your Majesty's subjects who pay taxes and share other obligations of citizenship.

4. Ever since Mr. Asquith, your Majesty's Prime Minister, has held his present office, the societies mentioned have sought an interview with him for the purpose of placing before him reasons why the Government should give facilities for a measure granting full political rights to women. To this end Mr. Asquith has on many occasions been asked to receive a small deputation of women representing the said societies, but he has always refused to receive any such deputation.

5. Moreover deputations of women have been chosen to present to Mr. Asquith in person at the House of Commons resolutions and petitions in favour of the proposed reform. Such deputations proceeding in a lawful, quiet and reasonable manner to the House of Commons in exercise of their undoubted constitutional right, have at the instance of Mr. Asquith been met by the forces of the police, denied entrance to the Houses of parliament and without fair cause have suffered arrest and imprisonment.

6. Mr. Asquith has been again asked to receive at the House of Commons a small deputation of women citizens representing among other bodies of organised women subjects the two societies named and he has replied repeating his former refusal. The deputation has notwithstanding decided to go to the House of Commons

and there repeat their request to see Mr. Asquith and submit to him reasons why the proposed reform should be undertaken by the Government. There are grounds for believing that Mr. Asquith will meet this assertion of right on the part of your Majesty's dutiful and loyal subjects with the same exercise of force as before and great wrong will be done to your subjects.

7. Your Majesty's predecessors have granted and your Majesty has confirmed to all loyal subjects the right of approaching your Majesty and submitting petitions for the address of grievance and your petitioners humbly submit that the subjects of your Majesty are acting within the spirit and substance of the Constitution desiring your Majesty's Minister on your Majesty's behalf, and in your Majesty's name to concede a like privilege to that which you and your Majesty's predecessors have ever freely granted.

Your petitioners would therefore humbly petition that your Majesty will, to prevent the threatened wrong, give such directions or take such measures as will ensure hearing today by Mr. Asquith of the deputation of women from the said societies
And your Petitioners will ever pray etc.

Many men publically supported the fight, including the authors Thomas Hardy, H.G. Wells and E.M. Forster. Retail tycoon Henry Selfridge sold 'Votes for Women' rosettes and went as far as to fly the WSPU flag from his famous department store on London's Oxford Street, where he also installed new windows of purple, green and cream (along with Liberty of London). There were men from all walks of life who were happy enough to publically support the cause despite the risk of ridicule and ostracising themselves from society, but the support of a politician was a coup for the movement. George Lansbury MP was a strong supporter of the WSPU and was able to voice his concerns within the House of Commons on the topic of women's rights, but he did so without the support of his Labour colleagues as they showed very little interest in what he had to say – to them women voting was not their way in to power. Lansbury called out the Liberal Prime Minister Herbert Henry Asquith for allowing the imprisoned suffragettes to be forcibly fed in prison. He called him cruel and contemptable and soon found himself slapped with a suspension order from the House of Commons for his conduct. Lansbury's argument was that these women were not putting themselves through the horrors of starvation and forcible feeding for the fun of it or to be famous, they had a cause and it was quite clearly so important to them they were willing to risk their lives in the course of justice. How could these well-educated supposedly well-respected men not see that this was wrong? How could they sit back and actively let this behaviour happen in their prisons? Lansbury's response was to resign his seat: he quite clearly felt he was going to achieve nothing in his current role so he decided to stand as a women's suffrage candidate, unfortunately he was unsuccessful. The suspension did nothing to deter Lansbury from his course, and he was later arrested and imprisoned for incitement after giving a speech at a WSPU rally. He took to the stage and urged the suffragettes to continue with violence and militancy, they had his full support and openly encouraged them to commit acts of arson. He was sentenced to three months in prison and like many suffragettes he endured a hunger strike and was released after a few days under the Cat and Mouse Act. Other men that were arrested as part of the campaigning also endured hunger strikes. Hugh Franklin was a Labour politician and ardent supporter of women's rights. After taking part in the 'Black Friday' rally in November 1910 he witnessed the police brutality against the women and was horrified by what he saw. He held Winston Churchill responsible for this and made him a target, following him on the political trail where he would heckle and be disruptive. Following one meeting, he met Churchill on a train and went to attack him with a whip. Franklin was arrested immediately and sentenced to six week's imprisonment at Pentonville. He would go on to be arrested and imprisoned twice more, once for attacking Churchill's home by pelting it with rocks, and later for arson after setting fire to a train carriage. He endured forcible feeding alongside his female counterparts and became the first person to be released on licence under the government's controversial Cat and Mouse Act in 1913.

These men were not lone voices. Despite the male suffrage campaigns not being as well-known as the female ones there were plenty of men on the campaign trail. Frederick Pethick-Lawrence, along with his wife Emmeline, were to become vital to the WSPU's fight. They were both supporters of women's rights and were introduced to the Pankhursts by Keir Hardie. As social reformers they were soon at the heart of the campaign. Emmeline became the WSPU's treasurer and by 1906 she had made them financially viable by organising fundraising events and finding ways to cut costs. Financially they were a lifeline: Frederick often paid the bail money and fines for many of the suffragettes who found themselves behind bars. Between them they saw that an organisation of the relatively small size of the WSPU was never going to have the impact it needed just by writing to MPs. The suffragists had been doing that for years and had achieved nothing, they understood the campaign had to grow if it was going to have any chance of success. The message needed to be spread so in 1907 they established and edited *Votes for Women*, a monthly newspaper (it went to a weekly publication in 1908), which offered discussions and details of upcoming rallies that was available at a price of 3d (later 1d when it was weekly) to all from street sellers. It was to be the mouthpiece of the whole campaign. Many of the women who went out to sell the paper were often subjected to verbal abuse and were even made to stand in the gutter at the side of the pavement lest they get arrested for obstruction, such was the vehemence and anger they aroused. The paper grew both in popularity and in size, with more and more information being covered in each edition. A new advertising campaign was launched and new permanent sale spots were established across central London, by the end of 1912 it was reported that approximately 33,000 copies a week were being sold. The Pethick-Lawrences were fundamental in making sure the suffragettes were seen rather than just heard. They suggested that rather than giving their speeches behind closed doors they now mounted soap boxes in the street and from the back of lorries in market squares. The aim of this tactic was to bring the message to the streets and directly to the people, passers-by could easily stop and listen, they were being opened up to a whole new audience and there was always the chance that a face in the crowd could be the next militant hero.

When Emmeline and Christabel Pankhurst were imprisoned, Emmeline and Frederick took on the day to day running of the WSPU. They ensured that events still took place and members were kept up to date with the latest news and developments. However, by 1912 things started to unravel. The Pethick-Lawrences were imprisoned, with Frederick serving up to nine months on account of his actions with the WSPU, and on his release they were summonsed to meet with Emmeline and Christabel in France. The couple had become increasingly concerned at the level of violence being used by some of the women, believing it was too much too fast and urged the Pankhursts to rethink their approach and change tactics. They suggested that Christabel return to the United Kingdom to be arrested, at which point public sympathy could be raised rather than losing it through violent acts which was very much a realistic risk. The Pankhursts were ruthless in their treatment of the Pethick-Lawrences. They advised them to leave the country and take no more involvement in terms of campaigning, and during this time new property was found to run the operation from. The split was confirmed to the WSPU members when the headquarters were moved from Clements Inn to a new property at Lincolns Inn Fields, just off Kingsway. The couple only realised this had happened when they returned to London to find the previous rooms empty. The rift deepened when the declaration was made that the violence and public attacks on the opposition would continue on both public and private land, with the aim of escape without arrest. Throughout this tumultuous time the Pethick-Lawrences remained dignified: despite Emmeline's desire to make the full details of the split public, Frederick convinced her that doing so would result in too much damage to the cause as a whole. They remained in charge of *Votes for Women,* which they published independently, and they continued to fight for women's rights. The treatment of this kind and generous couple was viewed by many members as being extremely heavy handed and unfair considering all the financial support they had provided the WSPU and how they had revolutionised the campaigning. Without them would the WSPU have made any impact on the cause? Christabel is said to have orchestrated their removal after taking serious umbrage with their suggestion that things should be done differently.

Publicity became increasingly important to the cause and the media played its part. On 10 January 1906, *Daily Mail* journalist Charles Hands coined the term 'suffragette' for the very first time. He meant for the word to be used in a derogatory manner, turning the cause and the women into small, feminine, insignificant beings, but the WSPU saw an opportunity to turn this into their favour and adopted the term as their own. The suffragettes and the media had a very fractious relationship, in general the press they received was not very favourable for them but they soon realised that if they wanted to spread their message nationwide they needed to make sure that they were front page news, regardless of if that was good news or bad news. They were depicted as neglectful women who abandoned their husbands and children to fend for themselves. Posters were created by anti-suffrage groups that showed children crying and men coming home to untidy homes, women were portrayed as neglectful, spiteful and downright dangerous. They were feared by the establishment because they caused a threat to the order of society, and it was deemed that these dangerous women had the ability to start a civil war with their militancy and cause severe unrest in the country.

It could be questioned if the militant campaign did, in fact, hinder the cause. The public were split as to whether or not they supported 'Votes for Women', but seeing people's homes destroyed and shop windows being smashed is not really the best way to bring people to the cause, and with the negative spin that the journalists depicted, the suffragettes faced an uphill battle. The men running the newspapers at that time were powerful and rich and did not want the social order to be disrupted, so their aim was to discredit women and the cause in order to derail their movement. It was not just the national press that had a vendetta against the suffragettes, the local presses also took the opportunity to vent their anger and dismay, as we have seen with the local reception to Edith and her exploits with the WSPU. It would be unfair, however, to label the entire press industry as being opposed to the suffragettes. Some reported fairly about their meetings and rallies, often commenting on how well received the speakers were and how the women conducted themselves with decorum and spoke clearly and concisely, thus ensuring their message was given over.

Despite the overwhelmingly negative reception in the media to militant action, the reporting soon changed to a more supportive tone when it was made public knowledge that the women were suffering at the hands of the government's instructions to start forcible feeding. When they printed pictures of women having feeding tubes forced through their noses, the public reacted with astonishment and disgust, and changes to the conditions the women were imprisoned under were amended. The *Preston Guardian* reported in February 1910 of Edith's treatment while suffering forcible feeding:

> The Governor, Matron, and doctor tried to weaken her resolution by telling her that the forcible feeding case had gone against Mrs Leigh and that the hunger-strike was at an

end. There was a pause for a few seconds while Mrs Rigby says she felt as if the ground were slipping from under her feet. Then she answered: 'In our opinion the judges of the law are wrong.'

There is a saying that a woman will do anything for a man but nothing for a cause. That belief has now been pretty thoroughly exploded – voluntarily, for a cause. The most delicately nurtured women have endured discomforts, trials and pains which few men would care to undergo.

You can almost sense the begrudging admiration and respect the journalist has for Edith and women like her, that sense of how important the cause must be if they are willing to undergo all this pain and suffering. Surely this was more than women being hysterical and emotional, this was a cause that was sweeping not just this country, but the world. Of course then, as is now, the press will report the news in the manner they chose to, knowing the reading populace would believe what they read, the readership at this time being wealthy men who opposed the campaign. The WSPU's own publication set about ensuring the truth was also being put out there, it was down to the public to decide which side of the argument they were on.

It is astonishing to consider that the relatively small size of the WSPU generated such a huge amount of interest across the country, but there was still much more they could do. They released newsreels of themselves working hard at their headquarters in an attempt to come across as a professional, well-run outfit. At the beginning of the campaign news was mainly spread by the newspapers, but as the new century dawned cameras were there to capture the speeches and marches. One of the most iconic moments captured was the tragic accident involving Emily Davison at the Epsom Derby, whose images would have shocked the nation. Whether you saw it as an act of bravery or thought she deserved what she got, there is no getting away from the fact that it was a horrific piece of footage that was out there for all to see. The newsreels meant that a whole new way of protest was now available. At a time when travel to London was expensive and took time for the women from the north, they could now feel part of the campaign through the silent newsreels that were shown in the local cinemas. The cameras were also there to capture Davison's funeral, which showed thousands of women all dressed in white solemnly following her coffin through the streets of London. Throughout the campaign one thing is clear: the suffragettes knew how to maximise their media presence. Whenever one of them was arrested and sent to trial they made sure the press was there to report every moment, all the times they were captured being man handled at the hands of the police the cameras caught it.

The spread of news regarding the campaigning was important at the time in order to promote the WSPU's message, offering them a platform to have their voices heard on a national level. Long gone was the calm demeanour of the suffragists. All of a sudden the front pages were full of stories and pictures of women screaming and shouting at politicians and being roughly manhandled by the police, all of this propaganda was an integral part of the success of the campaign as a whole. From politicians standing up in the Houses of Commons speaking out in favour for them, to the husbands who quietly kept home while the women campaigned, to those men who just quite simply recognised that the current voting system was prejudiced and did not fairly recognise the importance of women having their say, men were important to the cause and without them the whole message may have been lost. It is not necessarily fair to say these men were the deciding factor in women finally getting the vote, the women did that for themselves, but it is fair to say that men certainly offered them support and encouragement to continue the fight and supported them in many ways. From newspaper articles in the nation's press to the silent newsreels of the marches, the media coverage of the whole suffragette movement has provided a unique glimpse for us to look back and appreciate the movement in its glory. Indeed, there are many depictions of the suffragettes in many movies, television series' and books which all helps in ensuring they are never forgotten by future generations. Thanks to the role of the media, it has ensured the WSPU and its members have been immortalised and over 100 years later they are still inspiring women's movements to strive for a better future.

Chapter Seven

The Suffragettes and the Royal Family

By the time the suffragist movement had begun in the mid-nineteenth century, Queen Victoria had sat upon the throne of the United Kingdom of Great Britain and Ireland for nearly thirty years. She was one of the most iconic monarchs the country had ever seen and was to become known as the grandmother of Europe, with many of her children and grandchildren marrying in to the various royal houses across the continent. She was considered by many to be the figurehead of the nation, and someone the people looked to for reassurance in times of uncertainty. She gave her name to one of the country's most successful and progressive eras and with Victoria on the throne you can forgive the suffragists for thinking they may have stood a chance of succeeding in their attempts at change. The members of the NUWSS must have been confident that as a woman in a position of such power, she would understand and recognise their desire to improve women's lives and that she would publically support the need for change. They must have hoped she could persuade her ministers that women's suffrage needed to be discussed and considered. Unfortunately for them they were to be left bitterly disappointed, as despite being the monarch of one of the most powerful countries in the world and the empress of an empire where the sun never set, Victoria did not want to lend her support to the earlier campaigns for women's suffrage. She may have chosen to distance herself publically from any of the suffrage campaigns because she genuinely did not believe in them, or, she did not feel she could publically go against the advice of her government, but she was not going to be the ally the suffragists had hopes she would be.

Surprisingly, Victoria agreed with the majority of society that women belonged at home. It was her firm belief that women belonged to the domestic sphere and the business and political arenas were very much the male-dominated spheres, and that is the way it must stay. In her opinion, women had no right to be meddling with the accepted order of things, it had been done that way for centuries so why would that need to change now? She questioned why women would even want the vote, and what exactly did they intend to do with it, surely having the vote is a man's privilege and women should get on with doing whatever it was women should be doing, such as having babies and keeping house. To be fair to Victoria, she certainly practised what she preached as she had nine children and deferred to her husband, Prince Albert, on numerous occasions. She would often turn to him for guidance on business and for advice on the political issues of the day, and this proved successful when Albert was asked to help with the promotion of British trade and industry abroad, as this led to his greatest achievement, the hugely successful Great Exhibition of 1851 at the Crystal Palace in London's Hyde Park. To Victoria, her role as queen was extraordinary, and while there were, and had been, plenty of other female monarchs across Europe, this was to be considered the exception and not the rule. Women were not supposed to occupy this role, they certainly were not born with the expectation they would rule and they were not considered to have the requisite skills to govern a nation, or to be able to learn those skills. They were considered to be too emotional and would let their feelings get in the way of making rational decisions. Women were said to be governed by their emotions and therefore what a risk it could be to the nation if they let women have the vote – think of all those votes that could be cast based on emotions rather than as a result of making an informed choice based on the facts available.

At this time in the UK no female could inherit the throne if a younger male sibling was alive: she would be usurped and become a commodity in the marriage market. Thankfully this is now considered as unfair practice and the law has since been changed, male-preference primogeniture was replaced by absolute primogeniture. This meant that the birth of Princess Charlotte of Cambridge in 2015 made her the first British princess who would not be moved down the line of succession if a younger brother was born, which in turn meant that Prince Louis became the first member of the British royal family not to outrank his older sister. We can only guess what Victoria would have thought if she knew a female member of the royal family was able to outrank her own brother. To Victoria, women should not be aiming for such roles in life, and they certainly should not be trying to usurp the place of men either.

The death of Queen Victoria in 1901 brought her eldest son Edward to the throne. Edward VII brought a renewed optimism that at last, the stuffy Victorian era was over and the new, elegant, fun-filled Edwardian era was about to begin. Victoria had reigned for over sixty years and there must have been a slim glimmer of hope that a new monarch would bring fresh new ideas to the country: morals were looser and life was good, especially for the rich. Sadly, this was not to be as the new monarch was also against giving women the vote. The king was a serial womaniser and had countless affairs, despite being married to the beautiful Princess Alexandra of Denmark, of whom he thought very little. Despite having six children together he thought nothing of the shame and embarrassment his flings and affairs had on his long-suffering wife. He was firm in his belief that women were there for the needs of men, they were objects of pleasure and were to be enjoyed and Edward certainly made sure he enjoyed them. They most certainly were not there for intellectual conversation, women were not meant to be educated in the same manner as men, which was deemed unfeminine. Edward had showed early signs that his life was going to be full of pleasure, and he never let his future role as monarch ruin his fun. Sadly his mother saw this and had long worried that his life was one of debauchery and recklessness. He proved her right as he did nothing to change his attitudes or behaviour once he became king.

With all this in mind, it is not surprising that the king was absolutely against women's suffrage and he was angry that his Prime Minister Henry Campbell-Bannerman had supported the Women's Franchise Bill in 1907. He had no sympathy towards their cause and no time for what women had to say on the matter. Just like his mother before him, he could not understand why women wanted to be like men and copy their ways of life. To the king, men and women were different for a reason and it should stay that way. Therefore, it is unsurprising that the monarch did little to endear himself to the suffragettes and they were not going to let him off the hook so easily. They decided to vent their anger at the king in defacing the one penny coin by stamping their slogan 'Votes for Women' right across his face. This was a clever and yet simple bit of propaganda on their behalf: this was a coin in mass circulation and was used from everyone in society, from the poor at the bottom right up to the rich at the top. It was a stunt that provided maximum exposure, and at its very best it would have been seen right across all walks of life, and the length and breadth of the country. There was no escaping this slight on the king. They had gone straight to the top and in doing so they slighted every powerful man in the country. Of course, any slight on the king made the rich irate with anger, which further pushed them away from ever accepting and supporting the 'Votes for Women' campaign, but it got the message across that they were not happy with this current monarch's views on women. It was a clear act of utter disobedience and contempt on their behalf, but it was cheap to do and had a high impact. There is no direct affiliation with the WSPU to the coins, so we cannot say for sure it was done by them. They usually liked to make their links to acts of disobedience known, but whoever was responsible certainly created a talking point. How many coins they managed to deface is unknown and it is thought not many were actually altered due to the logistics of obtaining enough coins, although the coins used had been in general circulation for a few years.

The decadence of the Edwardian era was something people abhorred as it often meant the subjugation of women. This was a time when women were judged on their beauty and accomplishments rather than what they could offer the country in terms of ideas and service. The vandalism of Velázquez's *Rokeby Venus* by Mary Richardson at the National Gallery was a further retaliation by women in the face of such times and treatment. She slashed the painting from top to bottom in a stance against the treatment of Mrs Pankhurst by the government. Her view was she had destroyed the beautiful figure of Venus in retaliation to the government killing the beautiful Mrs Pankhurst slowly and tortuously in prison.

Thankfully not all of Victoria's children were against the suffrage movement, in fact three of her daughters were passionate about helping to improve the lot of women at all levels of society. Princess Alice was keen to improve nursing standards and was an admirer of Florence Nightingale. She founded the Princess Alice Women's Guild and they took control of the field hospitals during the Austro-Prussian War. Alice gave women the opportunity to be useful and to display the skills required in tending to the injured soldiers. She was a pioneer in many ways and after her marriage she moved to Hesse, a duchy which formed part of the German empire. It was here in 1864 that she founded the Heidenreich Home for Pregnant Women to offer support to those who had nowhere else to turn. The rights of pregnant women and new mothers was important to Alice and she caused shock, especially to her mother, when she decided to breastfeed her second daughter, Elisabeth. To Victoria this was just not acceptable as it was something a lower-class woman did, she even likened her daughter to a cow and cruelly named one in the royal dairy after her daughter. Thankfully Alice was back home in Hesse and there was not much Victoria could do about it, but their relationship was by that point under immense strain. Victoria was not an easy mother to get along with, she was very strict and immersed herself in the lives of her children whether they liked it or not. She was critical and treated them with disdain. Following the premature death of Prince Albert in December 1861 she became almost unbearable to them. The lucky ones managed to leave the clutches of their mother but motherhood remained a strange phenomenon to Victoria all her life, her view was that her children were there to serve her and no one else. It is astounding that any of her daughters grew to be princesses of conscience, with a desire to help where they could.

Alice's sister Princess Helena also displayed an interest in nursing and in 1870 she founded the Ladies' Committee of the British Red Cross, in which she played an active role in the recruitment of new nurses and the deployment of them where needed. Helena was so passionate about nursing that she became the president of the Royal British Nurses Association, which gave her an opportunity to oversee the training and education of the recruits. It was important to Helena that these self-sacrificing women were fully equipped to deal the sick and dying, and also that they had a fully recognised profession. Nursing was not just about women taking care of the ill, it was about recognising that women were putting their own lives at risk and that it took skill to do the job.

The most prominent of the sisters in terms of promoting women's rights was Princess Louise, who was a royal rebel and was never scared to push the boundaries, which as a princess were the strictest they could be. She was a talented artist and sculptor and actively encouraged women to take up these skills, despite it being a male-dominated profession. Louise was a scandalous princess and as rumours of an illegitimate child and numerous affairs circulated she remained strong minded and strong willed, and it was that attitude that made her mother finally relent to her having sculpting lessons. Education was important to Louise and in 1864 she set up the Schools Enquiry Commission, which found that secondary education for girls was seriously lacking and needed addressing urgently. So, in 1871 she became president of the Women's

Education Union, which was tasked in setting up secondary schools for girls, rather like the one Edith attended in Preston. Within the first three years the union oversaw the opening of ten new schools across the country. She also became the patron of the Girls' Day School Trust in 1872, the aim of this organisation was to provide day schools for girls but at an affordable price. Louise realised the importance of young girls getting an education and that it should not just be a luxury of the rich. While many rich families employed a governess to teach their daughters at home, there was a new desire to start sending girls out to school. Princess Louise also showed an interest in nursing like her sisters. It is commonly thought that the princess met with suffragists on multiple occasions to discuss their cause, but unfortunately she was unable to offer them her full public support due to her mother's opposition to their views. Despite being a princess she was still restricted in having her own thoughts and views made public, showing that women across the nation were stifled at every level of society, but when their own queen refuses to endorse their fight you knew it was going to be a long, hard battle. Queen Victoria gave her name to a period in her country's history that was synonymous with progression and advancement, but sadly that did not stretch to the emancipation of women and no one in power was progressive enough to consider the right to vote as a progressive step.

There was one princess, however, that Victoria did not quite have as much control over as she did her own daughters, and that was Princess Sophia Duleep Singh. Princess Sophia was the daughter of the Maharaja Duleep Singh and Bamba Müller, her father was forced to abdicate his throne to the East India Company and incidentally was also made to give up the Koh-i-Noor diamond, which now forms part of the crown jewels. Following his abdication, the maharaja made his way to Britain and to the court of Queen Victoria where he was well received and treated kindly, the queen even stood as Sophia's godmother. On a trip to India in 1909 Sophia had her eyes opened to the poverty and inequality that was rife at the hands of the British government, she also saw this back home in England and upon her return she joined the WSPU and joined the fight to win the vote. Initially she took a tentative steps as far as active campaigning was concerned, although she was caught selling the suffragette newspaper at the gates to Hampton Court Palace. Needless to say this was not well received and George V threated her with eviction from the royal estate. She certainly had a rebellious streak and was fined many a time by the police for various misdemeanours, but as far as she was concerned she had no vote and therefore she refused to pay up. In the end the police confiscated her property, only for her friends to go and buy it back for her, but she made her point. It will come as no surprise to learn that she was never arrested for her actions with the WSPU, the title of princess made certain of that. She was, however, monitored and followed to ensure she never made herself a martyr to the cause. Martyrdom was to fall to another ardent suffragette in the most tragic of ways.

The royal battle would continue when George V became embroiled in the campaign on 4 June 1913. Emily Wilding Davison boarded a train at Victoria Station, London, for Epsom to attend the Derby. With her she carried two flags, both in the iconic suffragette colours of purple, white and green. She intended to attach the banners to the king's horse, Anmer, as it rounded the last bend and headed in to the home straight: she was planning to get close enough so as to fix them to his bridle or by flinging it over his head. It was hoped the horse would cross the finishing line triumphant and wearing the suffragette colours. It was 3 pm and she had positioned herself at Tattenham Corner. When she saw the trailing horses approach, she ducked down under the safety rail and stepped out onto the course clutching her banners. Her attempt went disastrously wrong as just mere seconds after stepping out she was hit by the horse, which would have been travelling at around 30 miles per hour, and was flung in the air like a rag doll and hit the ground with force. The horse also fell, partially crushing his rider Herbert Jones, whose foot was stuck in the stirrup. He was dragged for a few yards along the track and was unconscious when he was attended by the course doctor, thankfully he recovered and was riding again within weeks, Anmer escaped injury free. Mayhem seemed to ensue for a few moments as those who had watched the leading pack pass now turned their attention back to the chasing pack and it took a few moments to realise what had happened. They rushed onto the track in an attempt to give aid to Davison and Jones, they were both taken to Epsom Cottage Hospital where surgeons operated on her two days later. But her injuries were catastrophic and Emily Davison died on 8 June from a fracture to the base of her skull. Her death was recorded as misadventure. This was a truly shocking incident and the king made mention of it his diary stating it was 'a most regrettable and scandalous proceeding... A most disappointing day'. Queen Mary described Davison as a 'brutal lunatic woman'. It was clear the suffragette movement was not going to gain the support of the current monarchs, although Queen Mary was to be a strong supporter of women's efforts during the war and she supported women in many new roles, including the formation of the first female police officers. Emily was sent hate mail while in hospital, including a letter which stated it was hoped she would suffer torture until she died. Many felt she did not deserve to live, with one callously stating she should be starved and beaten. These threats are extreme in any sense, but they are even more abhorrent when they were made because she had ruined their day out.

It has long been debated as to whether this was a suicide attempt by Davison in the name of martyrdom. There was speculation that she intended to pull the king's horse down, or that she merely wanted to attach a flag or rosette to it so that it crossed the line wearing their colours. Many think she was aiming for any of the horses, others are convinced she targeted Anmer on purpose. Some argued that from where she was standing she could not possibly know which horse was which until they were upon her. One thing is for sure, Davison did not divulge her plans with anyone before setting off for Epsom and she acted alone. There are clues that indicate she did not intend to die that day: she left no explanation note and she had a return train ticket in her pocket, along with a ticket to a suffragette dance later that evening. I am sure she had hopes of arriving at the dance the hero of the hour, having successfully tagged their colours to the king's horse at one of the most prestigious horse races in the world, a race which every level of society came together to enjoy. I personally do not think she intended to die on that racecourse. We look back now at the video newsreels of the collision with pure horror, the moment of impact and the sight of Davison's body being tossed about is truly sickening, and we can only feel pity for her. But at the time the media were less than sympathetic, with her sanity being questioned and many saying that if she had not appeared so fatally wounded they may have lynched her there and then.

Whether Davison had planned to kill herself or not, the suffragettes now had a martyr for their cause. They saw her act as courageous and commendable and they were determined that her funeral would be a spectacle not seen before. It took place on 14 June 1913 and 5,000 women, all dressed in white, were part of the procession from

Victoria to King's Cross, with 50,000 people lining the route. When it arrived at King's Cross, the coffin was placed on a train bound for Newcastle, from there it was to be transported to Morpeth, the birthplace of both her parents, for burial. It was reported that approximately 100 suffragettes accompanied their comrade's body to its final resting place, whether Edith was one of these women we do not know. Emily Wilding Davison's horrific death was a turning point for the militant cause and she instantly became the most famous suffragette, with her death being an iconic moment in history. The manner of her death has immortalised Emily Wilding Davison, and it is impossible to have a discussion about the suffrage movement without the sacrifice she made being talked about. Her suffragette career was the most eventful of the lot: she gave up her teaching career so she could join the cause on a full-time basis, she knew this was a fight that was not going to be won in a short space of time so she dedicated her life to the fight. She undertook many acts of militancy, including throwing stones at windows, blowing up pillar boxes and general obstruction. Her life came down to that one moment at the Derby in 1913 and it is for that act she is remembered for more than anything else. In total, she served nine prison sentences and suffered the horrors of forcible feeding countless times. Whether that sacrifice was intended or not does not detract from the fact that Davison was one of the most ardent and committed women of the cause. The suffragette's campaign was now at its height and back home in Preston, Edith was plotting her next move.

Chapter Eight

Life During the War

For much of the nineteenth century Europe teetered on the edge of war, with the balance of power so tenuous that it was inevitable that conflict would erupt. War was declared by Austria-Hungary on Serbia on 28 July 1914 following the assassination of Archduke Franz Ferdinand and his wife the month before. It was on 4 August that the United Kingdom joined the conflict, having issued a declaration of war against Germany following the invasion of neutral Belgium. The resulting chain reaction soon saw the whole world at war. The onset of war heralded a complete change to the lives of every British citizen. Men who were old enough were enlisted to the army and sent to the front line to fight. Approximately five to six million men left their homes, families and jobs in order to fight, with hundreds of thousands of those either killed, missing or injured. It is difficult to obtain exact figures, but it is clear that to lose these men over a relatively small amount of time was to have a devastating effect on the country and to those left behind. What is more, as battalions of men would be recruited together, whole towns could be decimated if that battalion was attacked.

Every single able-bodied man and woman had a role to play during the conflict, whether that was a soldier engaged in combat in the trenches on the front line, or those at home working in the munitions factories, docks or other crucial role. To get a job in a munitions factory meant good wages and an opportunity to be involved and connected with the war effort. Prior to the war approximately 200,000 women worked in the factories, but by 1918 that figure had increased to just under one million. With the Germans sinking boats carrying food supplies bound for Britain, it became even more important that the population be sustained from the land. As more men were being called up to the army the agricultural sector was now low on labourers, so, in 1915 the Women's Land Army was created. Thousands were recruited and it was down to these women to utilise the land and maximise it enough to provide plenty of fresh produce to sustain the country. The families who had men away fighting had to adapt to a new way of living, not only had they lost the main breadwinner, but the women now had to step into those roles to ensure there was enough food on the table to feed the family. The women at home also had to deal with rationing when it was introduced in 1918. Stretching the family's budget that bit further would require all the skills they had, but it was essential that there was a fair and even distribution of food if the country was going to remain strong enough to fight.

Women were now able to demonstrate they were capable, reliable and trustworthy, and even though many of the jobs that women did during this time reverted back to the men when they returned home from the war, they had proved themselves competent and worthy. In July 1918, the Reform Act finally enfranchised women over the age of 30 and who met the property requirements, of which Edith did. They were now finally eligible to cast their vote at a general election, yet it would take a further ten years for women to get the same voting rights as men. I am sure this would have happened at some point, but the effort they put in during the war on the home front certainly expedited that decision. To Edith, though, it was all won through their campaigning, and the government used the war as an excuse to grant the vote to women. As she explained,

> I'm certain we wouldn't have got the vote without the militants – at least, not nearly so soon. The war was an excuse to save the Government's pride. After withholding it for so long and breaking so many promises they were really bound to give in. When war came they made *that* the reason. But the truth is, they dreaded any more disturbances!

Whether or not the government used the war as a cover up for finally granting the vote, surely they must have looked back through the militant campaigning and admired the women's strength, determination and resolution and how they never wavered in their quest. The WSPU had an answer for every government action, for every broken promise and for every time they thought they stood a chance only to be thwarted at the very last. All of a sudden women had become important and valuable to the nation, after being told for so long that they were not worthy enough to vote, that their voices and opinions did not matter, they were now an integral part of the country's survival and that was a powerful position to be in. It is interesting to compare the posters produced during the campaigning years to those produced by the Land Army. Gone were the images of women being mercilessly mocked and ridiculed, now they showed them feeding the nation single-handedly.

In 1915 Charles and Edith made the decision to leave Winckley Square and buy Marigold Cottage in Howick Cross, just south of Preston, taking Mrs Tucker with them as their housekeeper. Edith had finally managed to escape the constraints of the railings of the square and the hostilities that her time there had been blighted by, and swapped them for a sleepy existence in the countryside. The cottage sat in five acres of land and came with its own orchard, which provided a bounty of apples, pears and plums, all of which Edith would make great use of. It had gardens, beehives and freedom: Edith could finally live how she wanted to without censure or scolding. She harboured no desire to become a town councillor and her campaigning days were over, so she decided her war effort would be based around agriculture and the provision of food for both her family and the local area.

With the move to Howick Cross and with all the land at her fingertips, Edith decided to join the Women's Land Army, which had recently been created by the Board of Agriculture to enable women to work the fields in the absence of the men who were away fighting. This is exactly what Edith intended to do with her newly acquired land and she embraced this role whole heartedly. She wore the breeches and farmer's smock that was synonymous with the Land Girls and cut her hair as short as she could, and she did this without repercussions – it feels like Edith had finally found her true and happy home. To get started she ensured the land was suitable for farming. Once she had satisfied herself that it was, and once she had given the exterior of the cottage a lick of paint (in marigold, of course), she set about buying a suitable horse, and a bay cob called Nutty and a pony called Bramble soon joined the swelling ranks of workers at Marigold Cottage. Edith was now in a position to start organising her contribution to the war effort. She and her friends recognised the importance of pulling together to do what they could to help, so they decided to set up an independent jam factory from their former meeting rooms in Glovers Court. Edith grew fruit and vegetables at Marigold and other women would collect blackberries and strawberries from nearby farms, which they would then take to their headquarters and turn into jam, along with cauliflowers and tomatoes to make into chutneys that they could sell on cheaply at a shop that had been set up in the Miller Arcade, a very early example of a 'pop up' shop. This was just part of the contribution that the women made and Edith now found that her life had a new challenge and a new focus for her good intentions.

Edith also found she had a passion for beekeeping, so she installed numerous hives on the land which led to a successful production of honey and she herself took on the role of beekeeper, complete with gloves and a net covered hat. All of this fresh produce, which was grown and nurtured in the soil at Marigold, was taken down the A59 to Preston twice a week for market days. Edith rode Nutty into town, who pulled his cart which was loaded with goodness. She was determined that only the best produce would be taken to market: anything that failed to make the cut was either eaten by the family or tossed into the compost heap. Nothing got wasted at Marigold and Edith ensured a full and wholesome diet was eaten. Goodness knows what people must have thought when they saw their one-time militant suffragette riding in to town pulling a cart of fresh fruit and veg, but Edith had never ever shied away from what people thought, right from her early bike rides around town to riding her horse. If something needed doing, she just got on with doing it. This was just part of the contribution that the women made and Edith now found that her life had to adapt, and like so many up and down the country, the Rigby family had to refocus their lives to accommodate the changes brought on by the war. However, I feel Edith encompassed this and like everything else in her life, she gave 100 per cent of her time and dedication.

Edith did much for Preston during the war and she made the decision to do this in relative obscurity. Like her father before her, she did not do the good deeds for recognition or personal glory, she did it simply because there were people that needed help and she realised she was fortunate enough to provide them with that help, which begs the question: how much more did she do that went unrecognised? I would like to think that the women of Winckley Square now acknowledged Edith and the good she was doing for the town. Considering in her suffragette years the aim was to be seen and heard, and when any deed had to be well documented and the louder and outrageous the deed the better, Edith did not like to take any recognition for her actions during the war.

The Rigby family settled in to life at Marigold Cottage. Charles was happy that his wife was at home safe and sound, with the threat of imprisonment and the horrors that came with it now over. In true

Edith style, she was keen for everyone to get involved in the running of the farm and every visitor was expected to contribute. She would have them picking fruit, turning the crops or cutting the grass: there were plenty of jobs to be done and everyone was expected to pull their weight, regardless of their reason for visiting. But as ever, Edith's personality won people over. She still had that knack of persuading people to get their hands dirty for a good cause and before they knew it, they had a trowel in their hand and they were praising the harvest. On many occasions there were WSPU tea parties held at Marigold, where those in the know would arrive early enough to fit in a weeding session and still leave plenty of time to enjoy the delicious food. Visitors, both friends and strangers, were always persuaded by Edith to help, which they were happy to do when they discovered the reward for a couple of hours' hard graft was afternoon tea with homemade bread and honey.

Charles was also happy to get involved when he was not back in town tending to his patients. He had retired from general practice and had become a locum for Preston's doctors, but unfortunately this had the opposite effect on what the family had hoped and instead resulted in an increase in his workload, so he spent the week in town and the weekends out in the country with Edith. He was such a kind and considerate man, who was dedicated to his profession so much that he never turned anyone down that needed his services. Edith had hoped that in his semi-retirement he may have taken a more relaxed outlook on life and would have settled nicely into cottage life, which he did and was happy to go apple picking and bring in the hay in the summer. His unfailing good sense of humour was put to use in the countryside, taking their whole new lifestyle with good grace and humour.

Cottage life proved to be busy for the Rigbys as the farm continued to thrive. Edith had learnt to drive by taking lessons with the chauffeur along Southport Road, and on a Sunday afternoon in the summer she would drive the short distance to Preston to pick up her Brook Street girls and bring them back to Howick Cross for some work on the farm and lunch. Despite it being many years since Edith had set up the Brook Street school, it was still important to her that she provided both mental stimulation and an education to these hard-working young ladies. When Edith set up the school she could not have imagined how successful it would turn out to be, and the fact that years later the women were still friends and meeting on regular occasions is testament to Edith's skills at bringing people together in the right situations.

In 1918 Edith helped found the first Women's Institute in Lancashire with the Hutton and Howick branch, of which she agreed to become the secretary. It seemed a natural step for Edith to take as their values were very close to her own and they seemed like the perfect fit. The Women's Institute (WI) was formed in Britain in September 1915 in Anglesey, Wales, and grew rapidly across the country. The purpose of the WI was to inspire women, especially those living in more rural areas, to grow their own food which they could then sell in order to boost the food supply chain while the country was struggling with the after effects of the war. The WI also had a prominent role to play when it came to fighting for women's rights, which the suffragettes had already started. In fact, many suffragettes became members of the WI so they could continue the hard work they had already begun. They even used the famous purple and green colours in their logo, reinforcing the links between the two female empowerment groups. Female identity was incredibly important at this time as it was the women who were propping up the country and it was reassuring to have the support of your fellow women around you. We may think of the ladies of the WI being Jerusalem-singing expert cake and jam makers but they were, and still are, so much more than that and what they offer to their local communities is invaluable. Within the first five years of their formation, the WI had already fronted campaigns for free milk for young school children and for more female police officers and midwives for the more rural communities. For over 100 years the WI has campaigned on a number of issues affecting women, and have worked tirelessly to fight for equal rights. Each year members are invited to discuss any topics they feel should be given a more nationwide platform. They will raise resolutions which are debated throughout the year, after which a shortlist is made of all the resolutions that require more awareness to be taken forward for campaigns over the coming years.

The list of all the mandates since 1918 is available to view on the WI website and it makes for fascinating reading. It seems inevitable that Edith should want to take part in this new organisation as it clearly focused on her areas of concern. What the ladies of the Hutton and Howick Cross WI initially thought of Edith is not recorded, but no doubt she would have made an instant impact on them. She would turn up to meetings riding her bicycle and wearing trousers with a short-bobbed haircut.

But as Edith had proved so many times before, looks and appearance are not indicative of a person's nature and temperament, and they soon warmed to her friendly personality. For Edith it was important that she was still able to offer support for the local community in such desperate times, and the WI offered her an outlet to do that. Before long they were enjoying talks, trips out and parties and Edith soon found herself judging the jam making and baking competitions. Most importantly, she enjoyed being among local, honest women for whom she felt she could engage with and enjoy their company. This part of Edith's life feels like it is her happiest, she is content at home in her cottage growing and providing for people. Despite being committed to her suffragette cause, she could not have actually enjoyed the prison experiences – no one could have – they were a means to an end, but now she was free of all that I think we see the real woman, and the person that Edith had always wanted to be. The fact she could live this life without the sneers and jibes of her old neighbours made it all the better for living.

By now Sandy was growing into a young man, but as a lad he had enjoyed a childhood where he could play out in the wide-open spaces that Marigold had to offer. He was a pupil at Trent College, a prestigious independent boarding school on the outskirts of Nottingham, which seemed at odds with Edith's educational beliefs, but maybe she understood that – charming as it was having to have places to run and hide in and things to climb on – a young boy must have a sound education behind him, should he want to achieve great things. He is described by his cousin Phoebe as being 'unusually shy', with a 'retiring nature'. It would be the arrival of another cousin, Herbert from Canada, which brought Sandy out of his shell. Herbert had been sent by his parents to live with his aunt Edith in order for him to get an English education (he attended Hutton Grammar School, which is not far from Marigold). Despite their age difference, the two boys got on well and were often seen together playing pranks on others, unfortunately no matter how hard they tried they never actually managed to cause Edith to fluster. They would perch on top of the cottage's thatched roof waiting for her to return from the fields, armed and ready to aim missiles in front of her, but with her cool demeanour Edith never flinched and the boys were to be left disappointed.

Being in the countryside fuelled a great passion for mother and son. Both took a keen interest in astronomy and would lay out in the fields in an evening to watch the stars and moon, and she would tell Sandy of the moon's power over the tides and talk of the different constellations in the sky. Once Sandy had left for school, Edith could share this passion with Herbert. He was to stay at Marigold until he left for the Royal Naval Training Centre in Dartmouth, but he often returned to Marigold for his holidays before he finally left England to take up his position within the Canadian Navy, where he rose as high as vice admiral. Herbert shared a very close bond with his aunt and would remember her fondly. As well as the working side of Marigold and its place as being a freehold to provide for the family and the wider community, it was also now a family home which allowed Edith and Sandy to sit among the grass together without fear of scorn or ridicule like they had back in Preston. The harvests came and went at Marigold, some good and some bad, but Edith was never deterred when a bad season failed to produce the yield of crops she had desired. Even when the bees developed a disease and all the hives had to be destroyed, she remained positive and got on with things by getting out the trusty old paraffin and burning the hives. She never lingered on a decision made on the farm: if a crop failed she turned it to mulch and replanted the next batch. She never had the time for self-pity and had to keep her production levels up to speed. She also ensured there was no waste to be had at the cottage: the land had to be worked constantly in order to provide sufficient produce for the family and trade.

Edith never went in to any decision without being armed with the full facts. We know that when she went to war with the local factories she also put in the groundwork first, building a case and her knowledge: buying and running the farm was no different. She knew she could not just start planting lots of seeds and tending an orchard in the hope it would all come together, it was vastly important to her to understand nature and how things came to be. As her interest in botany grew she enrolled at the Harris Institute in Preston, where she attended classes and went on expeditions. She learnt all the different components of flowers and how they all fitted together, but in true Edith fashion her quest for knowledge went much deeper than any lecturer could provide her. I am sure she could be a tricky student at times – with a thirst for knowledge like hers, the tutor must have sometimes struggled to keep up with her!

It was around this time that Edith started to take a keen interest in the Austrian philosopher Rudolph Steiner, who was to form a major part of her life from this point onwards. On one occasion Edith caught two school boys trespassing in the orchard and stealing apples, but rather than scold them and march them home to be punished by their parents, she invited them into her kitchen to enjoy the apples. To Edith, bad behaviour was partly down to poor relationships between parents, and their children and a lack of play time which enabled them to just be children. She is quoted as saying, 'Children need space as well as time for play if they are to grow in to happy and creative beings'. Her treatment of the two young boys comes from Steiner's belief that the moral and spiritual beliefs in children were just as important as their intellectual development. He called this new spiritual movement Anthroposophy. Born just outside Vienna in 1861, Steiner believed that there was a spiritual plane which was accessible to human beings and he taught his followers that their spiritual life was just as important as the life of their physical bodies. He taught them that through meditation they could achieve spiritual satisfaction. Edith took Steiner's teachings very seriously, to the point of learning German in the hope she would meet him one day to discuss his theories. She held regular meetings on Steiner and his teachings at her local St John's Ambulance buildings. Again, not wanting to just merely take an interest in something, she went the extra mile to gain a correct understanding and spent an increasing amount of time in Dornach to further her comprehension of his teachings. What she learnt while in Switzerland she brought home, and many of those teachings now shaped the way Marigold was run: no chemicals were to be used, no artificial products spread on the crops and no insect destroyed, regardless of its negative impact on said crop. Each creature had a part to play in keeping the order of nature in balance and absolutely nothing should be destroyed in the search for profit.

How much of these teachings she used in her parenting of Sandy it is hard to tell, but he certainly would have had plenty of open space and fresh air to run around in and I am sure Edith nurtured Sandy's spiritual side as best she could. Edith does not strike me as the kind of parent who would scold her child very often, rather Charles was probably the disciplinarian, not that we have any evidence that Sandy caused them any trouble at all beyond what a normal child would. Following his time at Trent College, Sandy later became an electrical engineer. He married a local girl called Hilda Sumner Stewart on 14 December 1925 at St James's church in Avenham, and according to their marriage certificate he was living at 62 Avenham Lane and was a motor salesman at the time. Their first child, a son, Charles Stewart Rigby was born 23 December 1926, and a second son would follow.

With Sandy now settled back in Preston, Edith's new-found passion for anthroposophy, and Charles needing to slow down, the decision was made to sell both Marigold Cottage and 28 Winckley Square and relocate to North Wales, where a new housing development was being built just outside Llandudno in a village called Llanrhos. It was the precise location Edith had yearned for: it was near the mountains and close by the sea, but was close enough to the town should they want to engage socially, and was the ideal place for Dr and Mrs Rigby to finally retire to. They picked their plot and building commenced. Naturally, Edith kept a close eye on the development and she made regular trips to the site to ensure that all was on track. While she was there she could dream of their future life which would finally bring peace, calm and relaxation. Unfortunately this was a dream that was to shatter before it had begun, as it was while she was on one of these trips that she received a message saying Charles had fallen gravely ill, and that she was to return home to Preston immediately. She left as soon as possible but the journey from North Wales was a long one, and Charles passed away at Marigold Cottage just an hour before Edith arrived home. Charles died of pneumonia on 9 July 1926 at the age of 68. Edith took the news of Charles' death extremely hard: it was one of the very few times that she lost her composure in front of others. It is difficult to state what her exact emotions were at this time, but anger must have been very high on the list. She felt that he had been overworked, attending patients even when he was ill: 'He was killed by the Preston doctors! When he was alive, they drive him to death, and when he was dying, they gave him no peace!'

Charles and Edith were married for thirty-three years, during which time his loyalty had been tested beyond any normal husband's, but he stood by Edith and he never wavered in his love and support for her. Their love for each other was deep and respectful, and despite the age difference they had a long and happy marriage. He is said to have had a great sense of humour and enjoyed spending time with Sandy and his friends. The bond between father and son must have been a strong one, all the time they spent together during the suffragette years strengthened their love and admiration for each other. He played his role as supportive husband to Edith without complaint, he was never a great lover of the countryside, or the sea, but to make his wife happy he agreed to move. He had vast amounts of friends and anyone who met him liked him and would do anything for him, as he would for them. I am sure many understood the difficulties having a wife as passionate and eccentric as Edith was challenging at times and he often found himself being mothered and looked after. His funeral took place at St James's Church Avenham, just seven months after Sandy's wedding. Edith's parting message for Charles was: 'Say not Good-night but in some brighter clime/Bid me Good-morning'.

We know that Edith was devastated at the loss of Charles. They were on the cusp of a new life, a life they could finally have shared together without outside influence from the suffrage campaign or patients, and you cannot help but wonder if she had any regrets regarding the constant interruptions in their married life. With her spending so many nights away, either campaigning in London or in prisons and then on the run, and him working so hard to tend to the sick, did she consider it all worth it in the end? The constant scrutiny she brought into their lives could not have been easy for Charles, but then neither could seeing his wife suffer the name-calling and abuse have been comfortable. To outsiders they were a mismatch, but their love endured and they were happy. However, it was now time for Edith to move on with her new life as a widow, knowing that her constant love and encourager was no longer there to support her. For all we know, Charles may have been the person that encouraged Edith to go that step further in her campaigning. What we do know for certain is that he was her soul mate, and the thought of a life without him must have caused her some anxiety. Edith was never a woman to hide or shy away from a challenge, and the next era of her life was going to prove to be just as fulfilling and rewarding as the others.

Whilst Edith was content with the quieter life following the end of the campaigning, it was not going to suit the likes of the Pankhursts and Annie Kenney. During the 'Votes for Women' campaign, these women had fought side by side and served time in prison alongside one another, meaning that they had ties that bound them to each other. They were reliant on each other, but soon after the franchise had been partially awarded many of the women simply drifted back in to their old lives, and post-suffragette life they all headed in different directions. Emmeline, the founder of the WSPU, embarked on a life of lectures and took many trips to America and Canada, even living in Toronto for a while before finally returning to London. Emmeline maintained an interest in politics and women's rights, joining the Conservative Party in 1926. She passed away in June 1928, just two weeks before the vote was granted to women on equal terms with men. Her eldest daughter, Christabel, who often comes across as the most ardent of suffragettes and someone who was willing to do anything for the cause, decided to stand in the 1918 general election on behalf of the Women's Party in Smethwick, but she was narrowly defeated. In 1921 she decided to leave the UK and went to America, where she joined her mother on one of her many lecture tours. She was made a Dame Commander of the British Empire in 1936 and passed away in 1958. She is buried in America. Lancashire lass Annie Kenney also hit the lecture circuit focusing on the war effort of the women. She told people how important the women had been in keeping the country going, married a man called James Taylor and had one son. She passed away in 1953 and her ashes were scattered on Saddleworth Moor by her family. Most of the women remained in contact with their local ladies and Beth and her family remained close friends with Edith until her death.

Chapter Nine

Life in Wales

Following Charles' death Edith decided she still wanted to move to North Wales, so she sold Marigold Cottage to the Yeadons (they had been living there with Charles when Edith was on her numerous trips to the continent in search of anthroposophy, so it was an easy decision to make). It was also an opportunity to finally repay Mr Yeadon for his support and help during the arson attack in Rivington. Along with the redoubtable Mrs Tucker, Edith made the move to her new home. The new house in Wales was a semi-detached property and it was decided that her younger, unmarried, sister Alice, who had been living up in the Lake District since their mother had passed away, would take up residence in the house next door. Edith's mother had died in Lytham St Annes in October 1923, having moved there following the death of her husband, Dr Rayner, in November 1916. So, at the end of 1926 the sisters relocated to North Wales. Edith named her new home 'Erdmut', meaning earth mother, and painted the front door purple, the fence red and the porch orange. We can only imagine the impact that had on this new neighbourhood, but I think it is safe to assume you would never have missed which house belonged to the eccentric Edith.

Alice was much more demur in her home décor choices: she named her new home Mount Grace, and we assume kept to a subtler palette when it came to the exterior. Why the sisters did not live together under the same roof we do not know, it may have been down to the space available, or maybe Alice felt living with Edith would be a tad too hectic for her. At what stage Alice decided to join her sister in the move is also unknown, but they were to be companions to each other despite their differing lifestyles. Edith was a wealthy widow: when Charles passed away his estate was worth the considerable sum of £6,624 1s7d. We are led to believe that Alice, on the other hand, had a significantly smaller income to live on, as she had never married and remained single all her life. The sisters' characters also differed greatly: Alice often felt bemused by her older sister's ideas and thoughts, but then Edith hated Alice's cat and never understood her need to have a pet, especially a cat. Edith was an animal lover but she had a strong hatred for cats and for this one in particular. Yet, sisters will be sisters, and Edith and the cat remained at a stand off until it mysteriously disappeared when Alice was away on holiday. The interior of Erdmut had a lot to live up to if it was going to compete with the exterior, but Edith did not disappoint her guests. This was the first time in her life that she had lived alone. She had gone from the family home to the marital home, but now she was free to do as she pleased in terms of decoration. She decided that each of the rooms should have its own name and theme, and the walls were covered in artwork of a more eclectic taste. The colours were bright and in your face, and the subjects unconventional. Now she was free to please herself Edith had well and truly embraced modern art, but despite the loudness of the walls and the earthly feel to Erdmut, the house was warm and welcoming. Edith welcomed her guests with the usual kindness and generosity and everyone was accepted. Alice, however, lived a much more modest life, the décor was more muted and the furnishings drabber. She visited her sister often for meals and to take tea in the afternoons, and it appears that the sisters lived independent lives but were still often in each other's company.

It was important to Edith that she integrated herself with her new home town and she quickly became a member of the Llandudno Field Club, which opened her up to many undiscovered wonders. The group would climb nearby mountains in search of ancient artefacts or stone circles and Edith would enjoy imparting her knowledge on what they found: her training at the Harris Institute coming in to its own. The sisters both shared a love of the mountains and music – Alice would play the piano and Edith would admire from afar, being a listener rather than a player – so they founded a new music club for the local community where they would arrange for different performances to be put on around the area. Edith's interest in Steiner grew and she took part in nationwide lectures. To her delight, Edith found there was a local interest to know more and after a year she set up an Athrosophical Circle in the town, even opening the doors of Erdmut up to hold their weekly study groups. Edith had a hand in putting on many of the lectures all across the north-Welsh area and naturally the lecturers were invited to be her guests at Erdmut.

With her spiritual mind very much catered for, Edith also took her physical wellbeing extremely seriously. She would rise early each morning at dawn to catch the bus down to the coast, where she then indulged in a spot of sea bathing – come rain or shine, she went. She braved the invigorating freezing Irish Sea on a daily basis in a bid to wake up her mind and set her up for the day, and would follow this with an hour of mediation back at Erdmut. When it came to meditation, Edith naturally followed the example set by Steiner. She would focus her gaze on one object and then imagine that object inside her mind's eye. Following her swim, she would then return home on the bus still wearing her sopping wet swim suit. She never took a change of clothes or a towel with her, she simply had a dip in the sea and waited until she returned home to dry off. As well as swimming, mountaineering had long since been a favourite hobby of Edith's and she now had a whole new host of friends to enjoy expeditions with. She scaled the summit of Mount Snowden on numerous occasions and was often climbing the local hills and mountains. On one occasion following a conference in Degawny, an expedition was put together for an afternoon climb over Crib Goch on Snowdon. Initially Edith was to sit this one out, she was getting older and was no longer as supple as she once had been, but at the last minute, not wanting to miss out, she changed her mind. Despite her age and her being unfit to take on such a challenge, she set off at her own pace and took the ridge with confidence, her follow walkers were much relieved when the summit was reached. This kind of determination proves that Steiner's theory of the mind being more powerful than the physical self was true as far as she was concerned. The problem with Edith was she did not know when to stop and once her mind was made up to take part no one could change it, which is very reminiscent of her suffragette years. Her self-belief knew no bounds and regardless of the concern she caused her friends and fellow walkers, she was always assured of her capabilities. Mountain walks can become perilous trips very quickly, sudden changes in weather can cause problems to even the most ardent and experienced of climbers. When some of their walks turned out to be rather tricky, Edith never wavered and never showed worry or fear, she just kept her course, took help when it was needed and focused her mind on the task. I am sure she caused her fellow walkers a few heart-stopping moments, but they quickly learned that Edith was more than capable.

Travel became a big part of Edith's life and in 1932 she decided to travel alone to Greece for a six-week holiday. She indulged in the local architecture and the ruins of Athens. She visited temples and marvelled at the archaeological wonders of the ancient world. In a postcard she sent home, Edith talks of the change to her plans due to an injury she sustained:

> A lovely day and I am to stay in with a hurt foot which late
> in its history turns out to be a very slight fracture. No man
> or woman should or *could* (!) get things just as they plan
> (what a fruitless world it would be!)

Needless to say, the broken foot did not keep Edith from her plans for too long as she was soon back on her feet exploring the ruins, and when things became too difficult, rather than pass an opportunity to explore, she hopped on a mule and continued her journey.

Her interest in archaeology came about from an earlier discovery that had been made at Bleasdale, close to where her brother Arthur lived at the time. Edith had been on a walk on the hillside when she came across an overgrown area, so she pushed her way through the branches and undergrowth to discover a group of old wooden posts. Excited by what she had found she visited a local farm and was told the story of its discovery from the son of the man who, in 1898, had made his own discovery. He told her how his father's spade had hit upon a wooden post and as he looked around it became apparent there was a circular formation in the ground. Excavations of the area soon showed up a large outer circle and a smaller horseshoe shape within that, while at the centre, two urns were found which appeared to contain human bones. Over time the site was planted over and was lost to the naked eye and was at risk of being lost for all future generations. Captivated by this story, Edith wrote to the *Lancashire Daily Post* in an attempt to bring it back in to the memories of the local people:

> Dear Sir,
> In a review of a book just now published on Woodhenge,
> by Mr and Mrs Cunnington, there is something of great
> interest to all Lancashire folk... who know Bleasdale.
> In this book, there is first an account of the findings of

Woodhenge in December 1925 by Squadron-Leader Inscall, V.C. He detected from the air finds of human workmanship, previously unknown. Then follows the account of the Cunningtons' most thorough excavation of the sire in 1926-28. Six concentric circles (or ovals) were found, into which columns of oak and pine were inserted, hence its name, Woodhenge.

Around the grave of a child (central) the long axis of the circles was aligned so as to mark the track of the Midsummer sunrise. This lies two miles to the south-west of Stonehenge, which it resembles in its orientation to the sun.

A few Prestonians will remember, about 1900, the finding of two similar circles in wood columns on a rounded hill, in the upper valet of Bleasdale. It was observed first by Mr Thomas Kelsall standing at the door of his farm above it, and he prepared a drawing and plan of the lie of the oak columns.

Will Preston people be vexed or pleased to be reminded that in the show-case of the Free Library, which purports to represent this [circle] there is no copy of this plan; there is no statement of the actual orientation of the sun - whether true east or to the Midsummer sunrise? With the cinerary urns, there is only a painting which is not accurate in its indication of the real position of the circles. It only shows the plantation of young trees planted then and which, in almost twenty years, has almost obliterated the [circle itself]…

I have just written to Professor Newstead, F.R.S., who described the recent finds of similar urns in Cheshire, to ask of there any other wooden circles orientated to the sun (as the Bleasdale Circle) known in England. Surely there are some people who will not let the wonderful heritage found by us… be lost, through neglect and lack of interest, to the generations of men who are to follow us?

Yours etc.,
Edith Rigby

Llanrhos
January 29 1930

Edith had outlined her desire to excavate and conserve the circle and she approached her brother to assist her. Naturally, a committee was formed to raise the necessary funds to get this project up and running. Edith approached the headmaster of Hutton Grammar School and she pestered him until he gave in and agreed to set up the Bleasdale Preservation Committee. He in turn then approached the people who would be fundamental in providing such funds. He managed to persuade the Earl of Derby, the Bishops of Manchester and Liverpool, Sir James Openshaw and many more to donate £5 each to raise the cash needed to get the excavation under way. They all obliged, some with more than the requested donation, and once the public donations had been counted they had enough to start the dig. A Mr and Mrs Varley were hired to lead the project, who would later become visitors to Erdmut. They started by removing the soil from within the horseshoe and when they removed each timber post the hole was filled with a concrete mix to mark the original layout. What they found was remarkable and it turned out to be the first timber circle to be discovered in Britain. It was the only one of its kind in the country and is the only circle where all the original timbers were still in situ. Some of the beams from the surrounding ditches were excavated and sent to museums across the country, including the British Museum in London and the Harris Museum in Preston. Edith had strived for this project to go ahead and had a lot riding on its success, so she made sure she was present throughout the dig, bringing a picnic and sitting nearby watching the archaeologists at work. I am sure she was keen to be more involved in the actual dig, but as this was a professional operation she kept her distance and left the discoveries to the experts. The result of the dig is that the area has been preserved and is now a local tourist attraction.

Old age was starting to creep up and Edith found herself having a stay in Preston Royal Infirmary in 1933 following a short illness. However, Edith being Edith, she was never going to follow a strict hospital regimen and was determined to have things her own way, so was soon causing a ruckus. She arrived at the hospital with her own personal library full of Steiner literature, which she insisted on having around her so she could spread them across her bed and read each book, immersing herself fully in each one. This was obviously not normal practice and the nurses battled with her daily to keep the bed clear, their argument was that her untidiness was bringing the whole ward down, which must have invoked memories of that confrontation back in Winckley Square. Edith calmly took up the matter with the matron and after a short stand-off it was agreed the books could stay. Never one to be constrained by rules and regulations, Edith took no notice of the hospital's does and don'ts regarding patients going AWOL, but that is exactly what she did. She somehow managed to get herself dressed and off the ward down to a waiting taxi to go and get a shampoo and set. How she managed to get passed the doctors and nurses we will never know, but even if they did challenge her I doubt they would have persuaded her otherwise. Upon her return, no one dared ask her where she had been, but they were relieved when the day came for Mrs Rigby to leave for home.

In May 1939 Edith was to undertake the biggest trip of her life when she and her niece Elaine embarked on a two-month holiday to America and Canada. Shortly before this trip Edith was diagnosed with Parkinson's disease, so she knew that this was a trip she needed to take now as soon she would be unable to. They boarded the *Laconia* in Liverpool and sailed for New York: their first stop was to be the Rudolf Steiner Settlement approximately 20 miles outside of the city. She was met off the boat and transferred to the centre, here she settled into a regular routine of lectures, gardening and cooking, she even learnt how to play the flute at the daily music lessons. In true Steiner fashion, she embraced the gardens and outside spaces, she also further honed her meditation skills, often at 4 am. After two weeks, she reluctantly left the settlement and headed back to New York and the Steiner Centre. While they were there, they took in some of New York's famous sites, including Broadway where they went to a show. She also acquired a love of ice cream and shampoo and sets in the American style. True to form, she also took a great interest in the lower classes of the city and those who plied their trade doing jobs such as shoe shining. Leaving her niece in New York, Edith set off for Halifax, Nova Scotia, to visit her beloved nephew Herbert, his wife Betty and their young children. Herbert had spent a lot of time at Marigold Cottage in his youth and later at Erdmut when he was on leave from Navy duty, so the bond between aunt and nephew was strong and this part of the trip meant a lot to Edith.

From here the group travelled to Ontario to stay with Harold, the one-time problem child who would play tricks on passers-by from the windows of their house in Fulwood. Much to Edith's delight, her younger brother had turned into a hardworking, kind and generous man who had married well and she felt comfortable staying with him and his family. She enjoyed her early morning sea bathing and spending time with her family, there were many excursions and some quality family time. Her niece had now joined them from New York and the group spent a lovely time together exploring the local region. When it was time to go home, the pair travelled by train to Montreal and spent a few days enjoying the sights of Quebec before boarding the ill-fated *Athenia* bound home for Liverpool (the ship was to be torpedoed by the Germans on its very next trip). Despite the sadness surrounding the end of the trip, Edith had enjoyed an enriching and fulfilling time and returned home to North Wales safely. One month after their return war was declared with Germany, and for the second time in her life Edith was to experience the country at war and life would change again.

Edith maintained her daily routine as best she could and continued to enjoy her regular activities, but her mobility was now seriously compromised by her illness. The tremors in her hand had risen up her arm, making her daily activities increasingly difficult. However, she would enjoy spending time in her garden or sitting in her lounge overlooking the poplar trees. She could sit and take in the views of the mountains she had once enjoyed climbing but were now way beyond her capabilities, regardless of her strength of mind. Her mind was still quick and sharp enough to continue her reading on Steiner and for her weekly study groups and lectures. As time went on Edith's mobility decreased to the point where she could no longer climb the stairs and could only walk as far as her garden, becoming dependent on two walking sticks to help her get around the house. If she wanted to venture further she was reliant on one of her visitors pushing her in a wheel chair the 2 miles to Llandudno. Sadly, at the same time the ever-present and ever-reliable Mrs Tucker suffered a stroke and was temporarily taken in to a nursing home. Unfortunately, Edith suffered a fall and broke her thigh bone, and to an already frail lady this injury was catastrophic and marked a serious decline in her health. She became immobile so her bed was moved downstairs and positioned so she could admire the surrounding rolling hills. News of her decline began to spread among her friends and family and she received many visitors over the last few weeks to say goodbye. The life of this once vibrant and eccentric suffragette who had experienced imprisonment, been a farmer and become a Steiner devotee came to an end when Edith passed away on 23 July 1950 aged 77, with her loyal sister Alice by her side. She was cremated at Birkenhead and her ashes were scattered at her request on Charles' grave at Preston Cemetery.

Edith had an amazing love for life. She was someone who was passionate and determined and was willing to fight for injustice even from a young age. It is interesting to consider what kind of person Edith would have been had she not been born and brought up on Pole Street. Her father could have housed the family in a much better residential area of the town, had she been brought up in one of those would Edith have still been Edith? Would she still have had a strong sense of the injustices shown to the poorer classes had she not seen it on her doorstep? Being brought up in the safety of a large home with her own set of servants may well have altered her view on life, it may have made her even fiercer in wanting to assist the poor. I simply cannot imagine her being the kind of person to ignore any request for help. Certainly a life on Pole Street brought the plight of the poorer working classes closer to home, but for me Edith was born with an instinct to help, it was in her nature to be kind and I cannot envisage a situation in which she would have turned her back on the needy. As for the suffrage cause, yes, she would still have been as active as she was, she may have been wealthy, but she had her eyes open to the world and regardless of where she may have been brought up and what experiences she had as a child, she was a doer, a fighter and brave enough for all those who felt they were not. She was also proof that it did not matter where you were born in terms of what you could achieve. Asquith commented that working-class women were not intelligent enough to have the vote, yet Edith was willing to stand up and prove him wrong by fighting for all those who she grew up around, all those women and young girls she saw from her bedroom window leaving for work at 6 am six days a week. She saw in them a determination and believed that they deserved to be heard – they had been ignored for long enough. Edith was never a proud woman and never put on airs and graces: she recognised she had been given choices in life that had allowed her to gain an education and a good marriage. A woman of her station could quite easily have settled in to a quiet luxurious life in Winckley Square, but that would have been the easiest choice and for Edith, the easiest option was never really the one she took.

She remained the kindest of people and one who showed consideration to others despite their station in life, and she was brave enough to push against the many boundaries that she often found herself up against and which had tried to constrain women like her. Her life was an extraordinary journey, from that young 12-year-old girl giving out her Christmas gifts to the poor, through to the suffragette who fought hard and risked everything for women to get the vote, and then through the Marigold years where the focus was still helping those left to cope when the country was at war. Her life in Wales was her time to enjoy the pleasures she wanted to, she was never put off when people belittled her for her dress or way of life, she simply listened to their remarks and moved on, the fact they had an issue at all was their problem to deal with, not hers. The name of Edith Rigby may not have stood the test of time outside of her home town and she may have been forgotten by historians who continue to write about the suffragettes and their fight, but to me Edith deserves to be remembered for the sacrifices she made in order to fight. She was a trailblazer, a fighter, a wife and a mother and thanks to women like her, women like me have the freedom and a right to vote.

Chapter Ten

The Suffragette's Legacy and Women Today

When we think of the suffragettes, what springs to mind? The Pankhurst women? Purple, green and white rosettes? Women being manhandled by the police at rallies or chaining themselves to railings outside Downing Street? Or Emily Wilding Davison being tragically struck by the king's horse at the Derby? All of these images are ingrained on our conscience, they are the very fabric of this country's history. They have been depicted in movies, on television and many books have been written and published about them over the years. It may have been a campaign that did not cover itself in glory at times, but it was a campaign that had a clear message and a very clear purpose. Looking back at the suffragette's campaign, do we deem it as a success? Of course we do, women were granted the vote in 1918 and then later in 1928 when it was given on the same terms as men. But was the militancy that was used reasonable? Can it be justified or were they nothing short of terrorists holding the government and country to ransom? Were women like Edith Rigby, the Pankhursts and the many other women from right across the country heroines or thugs? It is very easy to sit here and look back with hindsight and cast judgement over them and either applaud them or condemn them. There are many memorials across the country that are dedicated to the suffragettes: in 1970 a memorial was unveiled in Christchurch gardens in London, just stone's throw from Caxton hall. In 2018, to mark the 100th anniversary of the 'Votes for Women' campaign's successful end, a statue of Millicent Fawcett was unveiled in London. Underneath the statue are the names and portraits of fifty-eight supporters who helped win the vote. Sadly, Edith and many women like her are not included. Manchester is home to its very own statue of Emmeline Pankhurst, situated opposite the central library in the city, and shows Emmeline stood on a chair delivering one of her impassioned speeches. This is just a very small handful of examples, but there are many more dotted across the country clearly celebrating the women and everything they stood and fought for, regardless of the methods. We did not live in those times, but imagine if women today still did not have the right to vote, would we not be outraged and demand change? Yes, we would, and we would employ the correct forms of protesting, just at the WSPU did, but that is not to say we should condone the planting of explosives or arson, but things had gotten desperate. But, does that mean things are now on an even footing for women today in the UK? Maybe, in some aspects of life, but then in others equality still falls short.

The fight for women's suffrage was a long, drawn-out battle between the government and the women of Britain. For centuries women were seen as second-class citizens, being nothing more than a wife or mother, homemaker or cook. Society treated women at all levels differently, but fundamentally they were all supressed by men, as men were powerful both physically and in the eyes of the law. If you were poor you were expected to go out to work in the mills, factories or workshops while still keeping to your domestic chores once you got home. It was not much better for women higher up the social ladder either, in fact you could say it was worse as they had less personal freedom. If you were a lady from a wealthy family you were the property of the male members of your family, be it your father, brother, uncle or husband. From a young age you were trained in the requisite accomplishments that would make you a good wife: playing the piano, running a large household and delicate pastimes such as sewing and embroidery. You certainly were not educated to a standard that could be deemed too clever; women were not there to hold intelligent conversations with, they were there to look pretty and be demure at all times, no man wanted to be out witted by a well-educated wife.

To the head of the household, women were a commodity to be traded in the marriage markets to the highest bidder. Women were expected to marry the man chosen for her, and to her intended spouse, their prime concern was what financial gain a marriage to her could bring him, love had nothing to do with it. From a prospective husband's point of view, it was important the lady's dowry was of an acceptable amount, if he was lucky it would include land and/or money. Once you were married you were the property of your husband, you literally belonged to him: he owned everything you had regardless of origin, and it was now his property. If you were very lucky it would be a love match, or at the very least he would be kind to you, but if he was not then your life would be miserable. If you happened to marry a man with no feelings towards you your life could be very tricky indeed, and there was very little chance you could divorce him given that the divorce laws strongly favoured the man. He would take control of all your finances and any property you may have had now belonged to him. Your primary role in life was to provide an heir for your husband and obey him in all matters. So as a woman in the nineteenth and early twentieth centuries, you had many challenges to overcome. Of course there were expectations to this, lots of women married for love and their husbands were kind and considerate towards them, Edith and Charles being a prime example, although I do feel it took a woman of character to gainsay her husband. It was against these restrictions that drove the suffrage movement forward, the point had finally been reached in which women were finally ready to stand up and say no more, things had to change. Women had been supressed for far too long and they were not willing to take any more. Unfortunately, in order to make any changes they had to overcome their biggest enemy, a group of all-powerful men whose attitudes mostly followed the strict Victorian view on women, but the attitudes needed to change so the campaign for women's suffrage began.

As this and many other books will tell you, the campaign led by the WSPU was, at times, brutal. The violence, police brutality, subsequent imprisonments and force feedings were only a part of what the suffragettes had to endure in order to have their voices heard. They also suffered name calling in the streets, the turning of backs from your once friendly neighbours and the fear that every time you got up to give a speech in public you would be putting yourself in harm's way. But to them they had no choice, if they were to put their message out there they just had to make sure they shouted the loudest. It was not just the right to vote they were fighting for, many of the suffragettes were hard-working women who felt their contribution was being overlooked and at worse, being ignored completely. They were working in unfavourable conditions, paying their taxes like their male counterparts, yet they had no say on how those taxes were being spent. In 1913 the NUWSS published the below notice:

Why Working Women Want the Vote

Some Reasons Why Working Women Want the Vote

Because as long as women cannot vote for Members of Parliament they are not asked what they want, and they are treated like children who do not know what is good or what is bad for them.

Because only those who wear the shoe know where it pinches, and women know best what they want and what they don't want.

Because Members of Parliament must attend to the wants and wishes of those who have votes, and they have no time to attend to the wants and wishes of women who have not got votes.

Because laws are made which specifically affect women's work and the work of their children.

Because if women are working as dressmakers, tailoresses, printers, confectioners and laundresses, or in any factory or workshop, the laws under which they work are made for women without women being asked if these laws are good or bad for them.

Because if the laws under which women work are bad, women cannot have these laws changed unless they have the vote.

Because the vote has been given in some of our Colonies and has been of great use.

Because the way to help women is to give them the means of helping themselves.

Because the vote is the best and most direct way by which women can get their wishes and wants attended to.

All the above are perfectly reasonable points that needed to by raised, and are acceptable reasons for wanting and needing change. Of course there were those who did not want women to have the vote, mainly men who were frightened that a well informed and educated woman could potentially muscle her way in to a man's territory. Many men did not want their wives to be detracted from her duties, so they would dismiss the campaign and refuse to allow their wives to attend any rallies or demonstrations. These women relied on those who were able to take up the fight on their behalf, some would defy their husbands but the repercussions for doing so could be far too damaging to be worth the risk. Surprisingly, many women did not feel that having the vote was a good thing for the country. It was not all sisterly solidarity, as many liked their lifestyles and did not want anything to upset that. Such women tended to be from the higher classes and they were more likely to have been systematically conditioned all their lives to follow the instructions of their male superiors. Fear was one of the biggest forces against the suffrage campaign, fear from women that their lives would change for the worse and fear from men that women could actually hold any power at all. It was fear of the unknown and that is perfectly understandable, are not we all scared of an uncertain future? But fear was not an excuse to obstruct change, especially change that would benefit millions of people and in some cases, change people's lives altogether. All these obstacles combined, and the fact that many had tried before and failed, meant that the time had come for a new wave of women to fly the flag for women's rights.

As we know they were successful at last, following the hard work they put in during the First World War, which was seen as the pivotal moment that finally pushed them over the line in terms of recognition. But is that really the case, or, would they still have won the vote if the war had not happened? Obviously, that is a question we cannot answer, sadly the horrors of the war were real and affected many men of this country for years beyond its end in 1918. Not only did women take on the jobs of these men, but they were also there to support and nurse their husbands and sons back to health afterwards; the sacrifice they made was felt by many. There was certainly no indication from the government prior to the outbreak of the war that victory for women was imminent, but nonetheless the decision was made by all branches of the women's suffrage movement that they would cease in their war on the government. Millicent Fawcett famously said: 'Let us show ourselves worthy of citizenship whether our claim to it be recognised or not.'

In 1916, it was highlighted that many of the men away fighting had inadvertently lost their voting rights due to them being out of the country for a prolonged amount of time. The rules stipulated you must have a permanent residential address that you spent the majority of your time at, which was quite clearly impossible for those fighting on the front line. This opened up a brand-new discussion on the country's voting system and new legislation was passed that allowed all soldiers serving on the front line, regardless of age, the opportunity to cast their vote. But where did this leave women? Thankfully the sacrifices they had made had not gone unnoticed and they too were granted the right to vote, albeit with certain criteria having to be met. Finally, they had won. They had proved beyond doubt that they were worthy enough to have their say, they had served their country in its time of need and now they were being rewarded. But is reward the right choice of word here? Surely it was their right as a citizen of a democratic country that they should have had that right from the same time as men. By claiming the government had rewarded the women for doing something special dismisses the impact they had during the war. Women did not approach the war thinking that it was an ideal opportunity to get one over on the government, it was not something to be done just to win a prize. Women lost husbands, sons, brothers and uncles to the fighting, the sense of helplessness they must have felt would have been overwhelming so they did what they did because they had to, and not because they wanted the vote.

Despite the success of being granted the vote in 1918, it would take until the Equal Franchise Act of 1928 to put men and women on an equal footing in terms of voting rights, when anyone aged 21 and over had the right to have their vote counted. So, they had done it, they had achieved what in 1832 Mary Smith had set out to achieve when she presented Henry Hunt MP with the first suffrage petition. But what about now? How do women today feel about their right to vote? Do they support the militant action of the WSPU? More importantly, how much further do we have to go until we have universal suffrage and until the gender gap has closed in all areas of life?

I decided to ask a group of women of all ages from across the United Kingdom these questions. My first question was whether they felt that having the vote was a privilege or whether it was their right. Over 55 per cent said it was their human right as a person living in a democratic society that they should have the right the vote, some agreed that it was both a right and a privilege, as until universal suffrage is achieved we should consider it a privilege that we have been granted the opportunity to cast our votes. What about whether or not they feel obliged to vote at election time? I was interested to know if there was any element of guilt among women if they did not use their vote when given the opportunity to. Or, whether the suffragettes had fought for them to have the choice of whether they choose to use their vote or not. It was a tight result with 38 per cent of women feeling they had a choice as to whether or not they exercised their right to vote. My opinion is that the suffragettes fought tirelessly for women to be able to go to the polling station on election day, but it is their choice and they should not feel obliged to. The suffragettes represent freedom for women to make their own decisions in terms of who they may vote for and also whether they choose to exercise their right to cast their vote.

In the current political climate in the United Kingdom, many women have expressed issues regarding a lack of choice in terms of a political party they would actually want to vote for. So, rather than abstain from voting altogether, many women cross through the ballot paper, therefore ensuring it has been counted even if it is as a spoilt ballot. I am not advocating that women alone do this, as I am sure many men may do this as well. The next question focused on the suffragette campaign itself, and whether or not the militant action taken was justified or not. From a modern-day point of view, I thought this would be a difficult question to answer given the current terrorist threat we live under, but surprisingly 72 per cent of those asked agreed that it was justified. The common feeling was that they had no option left to them as the peaceful protests had no effect whatsoever. That being said, many felt uncomfortable having this view point. It is always worth mentioning that while some of the criminal acts they used were very serious, there was never an intention of causing harm to life. It was never intended that any member of the public was put in danger, the only ones who were in danger were the suffragettes themselves and many of them were willing to die for their cause. Having established how modern-day women feel about the suffragettes and their cause, I turned my attention to how they feel they are classed in today's world. I questioned if they still felt like second-class citizens in today's society and in which areas this was the case. The results showed that 57 per cent felt they were still classed as an inferior member of society, with just over 36 per cent saying the areas this felt most relevant is in regards to equal pay, followed by day to day sexism. It is easy to say that modern-day women have a much better standing in society today, but it is quite clear that there are elements that we still lag behind in, and that a man should receive a higher wage than a woman for doing the same job with the same level of experience is inexcusable and unjustifiable. Yes we can now vote, but there are still many ways in which a woman's lot trails behind that of men. The way society views women remains rooted in the nineteenth century, with women still being viewed as the homemakers and carers. For the most part it is the female members of the family who tend to the welfare of the youngsters and aging parents and grandparents, and it is often assumed that that is ok, or is expected of them.

Edith and her fellow suffragettes proved that women, both then and now, have the ability to force change if they are willing to fight for it. Things have changed dramatically over the past 100 years for women, but there is still work to be done. We are still seeing inequality against women and a new battle started in 2010 when the government announced that women born in the 1950s would see their retirement ages increased. The government's changes to their retirement dates meant that they were given insufficient time to make alternate arrangements, which led to many women being financially disadvantaged by the scheme, intended to bring women in line with men. The accusation that the government had acted unlawfully towards approximately 3.8 million women was rejected by the High Court in October 2019 when it was declared that the changes did not discriminate on the grounds of sex because the new legislation did not treat women any less favourably as it does men, instead it redresses the balance of equality between the sexes. We can agree that the state retirement age should be equal, but for this specific group of women who sacrificed years of their working lives to have children and raise a family, and for those who suffered unequal pay, it is questionable as to whether this has been handled correctly by the British government. Should these women not be compensated for lost earnings and for the mishandling of the transition? Surely it would have been more prudent to have a more transparent transition period, but just as 100 years prior, the women appear to have been fed lies and given false hope by the government. In January 2020 the group were granted permission to take their case to the court of appeal, so there does remain hope that the right decision will be made and this group of women will finally have the inequality rebalanced.

As long as there is a need to battle for equality there will always be a new wave of brave women who will shout up and fight. Many women congregated outside the High Court dressed in the suffragette colours of purple, green and white, the acknowledgement of these famous colours when worn by women is strikingly powerful and the message they send it clear for all to see. Women want and deserve equality regardless of what the government may think, and using the cost of redressing the balance as an excuse to ignore these women is cowardly. I think it is right and proper that women continue to hold the suffragettes in high esteem. They were trail blazers and are the very reason that a woman today can walk into the polling station with her ballot paper in hand and cast her vote for a say on how their country is run. For that, we thank them. The subjugation of women in other areas must stop. Why is it ok to cause countless numbers of women untold stress and worry because the government failed to correctly handle the new retirement process? Once again the government of the United Kingdom has let down its female population.

There were many women who supported the fight for women's suffrage across the years. Along with the likes of Millicent Fawcett, the Pankhursts and the other suffragettes and suffragists, there were women who were both pioneers and supporters of women's rights. Prior to the start of the suffrage campaigns of the nineteenth century, the eighteenth century saw its own campaign to better the rights of women. Those such as Mary Wollstonecraft began to raise awareness of the political and social injustices against women. It was Wollstonecraft's view that women were only considered inferior to men due to the lack of education they received in comparison to their male counterparts, it was nothing to do with the genetic make-up of women that made them any different and therefore both men and women should be treated as social equals. This theory is explored in her most famous work *A Vindication of the Rights of Women*, which was published in 1792 and is considered to be one of the most important texts ever written in relation to women's right. Mary's daughter, Mary Shelley, was to become a victim of male dominance in her field. When her masterpiece *Frankenstein* was published in 1818, no one was willing to believe it was solely the work of a woman, so they attributed her husband, the poet Percy Bysshe Shelley, as being the novel's co-author. It is not to say he did not make any contribution to the novel, but further investigation of Mary's notes would suggest his involvement was not as comprehensive as was first thought. It was Wollstonecraft's work that cemented her place as one of the first feminist writers to publicly make a stand for women's rights. It was not just the right to vote that women were fighting for, it was for women's rights right across the whole spectrum of society.

Other prominent Victorian women such as Florence Nightingale also supported women's suffrage, but her main argument was that women should be able to have access to any career they wished to. As nursing is a caring profession, many thought women should undertake the role without pay as caring is something women do naturally, but for Nightingale these women deserved more, they deserved the recognition for the difficult and skilled job they did. As the pioneer of nursing she felt that women were being subjugated in society and that they had every right to earn own their own money and their own property, independent of any man. The author Virginia Woolf was also an active campaigner for women's rights and was a member of the People's Suffrage Federation. She wrote about the subjugation of women and the sexual inequality in her writings, with her novel *A Room of One's Own* pushing at the boundaries of accepted literature of the time. Woolf was lucky that she was accepted as a female author who could write and publish in her own name, but it was not that much earlier that female writers had to assume a male penname in order to stand any chance of achieving success. Probably the most famous examples of this are the Brontë sisters, who assumed the names of Currer, Acton and Ellis Bell, and Mary Ann Evans, otherwise known as George Eliot. Charlotte and Anne Brontë were forced to visit London themselves in order to prove their identity with their publisher to make them see that it was women who were writing these novels, as it was assumed women were not capable of writing stories about love, romance and madness. Woolf also recognised that much more needed to be done and that women were going to need to win more than the vote if they wanted to be accepted on equal terms with men.

Women in the modern day are still campaigning for women's rights across the world, and there are many strong female role models today that young women can look to for inspiration. There are many women who have proved that gender should not be, and is not, a barrier to their work and lives. Love or loathe her, Margaret Thatcher proved that being a woman was not going to be a hurdle to her when in 1979 she became the first female prime minister of the United Kingdom, just over fifty years after women had fully won the vote. She would hold the post for eleven years, making her the longest-serving prime minister of the twentieth century, so she must have been doing something right. But she was a controversial leader and many of her decisions are still debated today as to whether or not they were good for the country. Being in a role as powerful as this was never going to be easy for a woman: she not only had to succeed in the role in the first place but she had to go above and beyond in that role to prove she was worthy of doing the job. No man has to do this, they can simply assume the role and get on with things, but for a woman, she is always identified by her gender first and her abilities second.

A woman in a role of power is always going to be overly scrutinised. Any wrong decision made or wrong turn taken and she will be vilified and proclaimed not good enough for do the job, simply because she is a woman. Thatcher was not called the Iron Lady for nothing and was never an outright campaigner for women's rights, in fact she did nothing to help promote the rise of women in government. In an interview with *The Guardian* in 2013, journalist Jenni Murray discusses an earlier interview with Thatcher in which the role of women was discussed. Thatcher claimed 'a woman must rise through merit, there must be no discrimination', which is, of course, absolutely correct, but Thatcher was not a woman for women, she backed equal rights but did very little to promote the lot of women. 'I didn't get here by being a strident female, I don't like strident females' was her standpoint when asked how she felt being the first female prime minister. If the women of the United Kingdom thought they had someone who would listen to their concerns they were very much mistaken: to Thatcher, both sexes were equally important and that is how she treated them. Despite this demeanour and her outward attempts to distance herself from her gender, women did see her as a role model and proof that women could achieve anything they wanted to if they were willing to put in the hard work and overcome the stigmas attached to their gender. It would take a further twenty-six years for another woman to succeed to the role of prime minister, when in 2016 Theresa May took over as the leader of the country. The lack of female representation within the Cabinet is an issue that will take time to rectify, but women have proved they are capable of holding positions of high office and it is hoped over time the disparity between men and women will become more equal.

Does this mean women are put off a career in politics and there are not enough women to challenge the posts? Maybe, but women have never had equal opportunities in the job market simply because they leave to have children. It is often women who then sacrifice their careers to bring the children up, when they are ready to return to the workplace, things have often moved on and working mums can feel left behind. Despite changes being made in the workplace, men are often the breadwinners and women the carers, so does this need to change? Well yes, it does, and it is. The times of assuming women are one thing or another (and men for that matter) are waning and the lines between gender-stereotyped roles are becoming ever increasingly blurred.

Across the pond in America we are still awaiting the election of the first ever female president. However, Michelle Obama used her position as first lady to publicly campaign for the right for young girls and women worldwide to receive an education. She often used her speeches to further awareness surrounding gender equality, and she was adamant that those kinds of conversations must continue to be openly discussed regardless of who that may upset and make feel uncomfortable. The Obama administration did much to promote women's rights within America, and in March 2009 President Obama oversaw the implementation of the White House Council on Women and Girls, which ensures that at the heart of every federal agency decision is the wellbeing and needs of women and girls. Obama's administration also implemented many initiatives that support and encourage gender equality for women.

There are many movements and activists across the world that continue to campaign on behalf of women, and Tarana Burke's #MeToo movement went worldwide in 2017. The movement gained a huge online following in the aftermath of the Harvey Weinstein scandal and it provided women with an opportunity to empower themselves through unity against sexual abuse that women face. This movement is now synonymous with women's power and provides them with a force to show solidarity with each other and with those who have been victims of sexual violence. In this modern day, social media has made it much easier to follow and support these campaigns: the use of a simple phrase now has the ability to give the most powerful of messages. Of course, it is not just older women that have the capability to promote change. One young girl who stands out as one of the female world's inspirations is Malala Yousafzai. She hit the headlines in 2012 when she was shot by the Taliban while on the bus on her way home from school in Pakistan. She adamantly maintained that she had a right to an education and that she should be able to attend school, despite female education at that time being banned under the Taliban's regime. Following her recovery and move to the United Kingdom, she continues to fight for young girls to have the right to an education and in 2014 she became the youngest recipient of the Nobel Peace Prize. Teenager Greta Thunberg has been a huge advocate for climate change, and the young Swedish teen has held meetings with some of the world's most powerful leaders, meetings that would daunt many people but she has the confidence within herself to attend and covey her message clearly. She has taken her female empowerment and used it to her advantage, and in turn to the advantage of the whole world.

The names mentioned here are just a tiny fragment of the women who are powerful enough to speak openly on women's rights, but it is not just about fighting for women's rights that is important here, it is about having a female figure that women today can look up to and be inspired by. There have been many women throughout history that have given women the belief that they are just as capable as men: Joan of Arc, Elizabeth I, Catherine the Great and Marie Curie are just a handful of women that excelled in their lives and proved what women are capable of doing when given the opportunity.

Of course, I cannot end this discussion without mentioning our current monarch, Elizabeth II. She has sat on the throne of our country for over sixty years and is now considered the most recognisable woman, if not person, in the world. She has offered stability in times of uncertainty, and at the age of 94 has fulfilled her duty since the ascending to the throne in 1952. Many have stood up and fought for women's rights, at times they have been ridiculed and shot down, but ultimately women are strong and they get up and start again. Female solidarity is at its strongest when women come together and fight the injustices levelled against them.

Despite these inspiring women there is so much more that still needs to be said, and it is shocking to think we are still saying the same words the suffragettes declared over 100 years earlier. They may have won the vote in the UK, but the equality between men and women remained an issue as much as it does today. The gender pay gap is still a talking point, and despite strides forward being taken to amend this woman still do not earn the same amount of money that men do for the same work. Women can be penalised for taking maternity leave in terms of promotion prospects, bonuses and job opportunities. You are punished on the one hand in your career for having children, and yet you are stigmatised in society if you do not have children. Society cannot seem to handle those women who have made the conscious choice not to have children: they are seen as unfeminine and failing in their duty as a woman. Yet, as women today we have the right to choose whether we want children. The reasons are varied and will be different for each woman, but everyone who has made that life choice does so because she can. One area which is no longer a concern is that all children in the UK are entitled to an education from a young age. The days of children working instead of learning are long gone here, but sadly that cannot be said of everywhere. As hard as we might try to believe that things have changed completely, there are still some social stigmas attached to daily life. It is still the view that women are the homemakers and the baby raisers. It is not as one sided as it was, but the majority of family care is provided by the women and that is expected as the norm. Employment law states that a woman should not be discriminated against in terms of her having children or the ability to have children, and should be judged solely on her merits for the role in which she is applying for, but sexual discrimination is still within the workplace and remains one of the biggest areas of inequality today.

There are other aspects of life that are still considered to be either male or female dominant, and that is most apparent in sport. Football is still very much a male-dominated sport both on the terraces and in terms of playing, although it is good to see a shift being made to make women's football more mainstream and for it to be taken more seriously. During the First World War, a group of women started working for a munitions company in Preston called Dick, Kerr & Co. These women joined together to form a football team, and despite female football being classed as inappropriate it was decided that the exercise would do them good and would boost morale. Dick, Kerr Ladies team was formed and soon they were playing to thousands at Deepdale, Preston. They were good, in fact they beat the men's factory team and went on to dominate the game. Unfortunately for them, the FA took offence that a women's team could draw the crowds they did and it was deemed too popular, so they banned women's football from any of their member grounds in December 1921. They hid behind the reasoning that football was an unsuitable game for women, they were deemed as not being physically capable of playing the game but it was obvious to all that the FA did not want them to outshine the men's teams. Just less than a year after the ban a game was held at Goodison Park in which over 53,000 people were in attendance. It remained the highest ever attendance for a women's game for over ninety-eight years until 2019, when 77,768 people turned up to watch England's women team at Wembley. It took until July 1971 for the FA to recognise women's football again, but sadly the damage had already been done. Back in those days teams like Dick, Kerr Ladies could fill the biggest grounds in the country, but due to the short sightedness of the men at the FA they had now lost all their support, facilities and talent. The game may never achieve the same level of success as the male game, but it is important that women are acknowledged as having a role within the sport.

The shift towards more of a female presence on television with regard to commentary and punditry shows us that the knowledge is there and we can no longer assume that only men have an opinion on the sport. On the terraces when you look around the crowd it is still very much dominated by men, and one of the women I interviewed commented that she often gets asked if she knows anything about football and did she need the rules explaining to her. That arrogant presumption by men who think just because she is a woman she has no clue about the game is sadly still with us. There have been many instances in recent years in which apologies have had to be made to female competitors as they are not judged on their talent but on their looks. A male commentator recently made a remark about a female athlete's appearance, regardless of the fact it had no bearing on her sport or performance. How and why he felt the need to make these comments is baffling, and why he felt it was appropriate to pass judgement on someone else's appearance proves that sexism still exists today.

The battle to win the vote was fought against the backdrop of a country that had undergone a huge transition from small island nation to a technologically advanced powerhouse. The industrial revolution changed the lives of many people in the United Kingdom, suddenly jobs were available and not just for men, women were finally getting a taste of what life could be like away from the domestic setting. They were finally earning their own money and while some of that had to be given over to the household, there was still a little left over for them to spend as they wished. Women may have been working long hours in often dangerous conditions, but a new era had begun where women were breaking free of the restraints of a society that had kept them at the beck and call of men. Winning the right to vote was the natural next step for women to take in their quest for equality: they had been liberated from the home and the time had come for them to be liberated in terms of having their say. History has shown us that when women are faced with a challenge to their gender they will stand up and fight for their rights. Of course, women today cannot use the militant actions used by the suffragettes. Setting a bomb off in any circumstance and for any cause is not acceptable and there is no easy way to avoid paying your taxes, but that does not mean women can be underestimated when it comes to campaigning for equality.

Women today, especially younger women, are empowered and feel they are strong enough to speak, they will not be quietened and put off from having their say. In the digital age in which we live, it is becoming ever easier to start spreading the messages for change and that can be done on a worldwide scale with the push of a button – you can create a movement in seconds and can gain thousands of supporters in minutes. The fight for votes was a worldwide campaign with each country mounting its own suffrage campaigns, and while we do not have complete universal suffrage, we must acknowledge that the fight the suffragettes fought was both important to them, but also to this country as a whole. Whether you agree with the militant stance or not, it was a fight that needed to be fought, and thanks to the resolute, hardworking and reliable women that helped the country through one of its darkest periods, we now have the right to go to the polling station to have our say. Of the women I interviewed, each one of them agreed that the suffragettes were right to do as they did, some had reservations but they understood that action was needed and women today are stronger and more powerful than they ever have been. Emmeline Pankhurst, her daughters and women like Edith Rigby could never have imagined how far women have come since their militant days, and it is important that those women are remembered for what they achieved, for it was monumental.

Bibliography

ATKINSON, Diane, *Rise Up, Women!* (Bloomsbury, 2018)

ATKINSON, Diane, *The Suffragettes in Pictures* (The History Press, 2010)

DENNISON, Matthew, *Queen Victoria: A Life of Contradictions* (William Collins, 2013)

HESKETH, Phoebe, *My Aunt Edith: The Story of a Preston Suffragette* (Lancashire County Books, 1992)

JOHNSON, Keith, *Secret Preston* (Amberley Publishing, 2015)

JOHNSON, Keith, *Preston Remembered* (The History Press, 2011)

LEWIS, Helen, *Difficult Women: A History of Feminism in 11 Fights* (Jonathan Cape, 2020)

MARLOW, Joyce, (Editor), *Suffragettes: The Fight for Votes for Women* (Virago Press, 2015)

MIDORIKAWA, Emily, and **SWEENEY**, Emma Claire, *A Secret Sisterhood: The hidden friendships of Austen, Brontë, Eliot and Woolf* (Aurum Press, 2017)

MURRAY, Jenni, *A History of the World in 21 Women* (Oneworld Publications, 2018)

MURRAY, Jenni, *Votes for Women!* (Oneworld Publications, 2018)

PANKHURST, Emmeline, *My Own Story* (Vintage, 2015)

PANKHURST, Helen, *Deeds Not Words: The Story of Women's Rights – Then and Now* (Sceptre, 2019)

PENGUIN BOOKS, *The Suffragettes* (Penguin Classics, 2016)

The Definitive Visual Guide History of Great Britain & Ireland (Dorling Kindersley, 2012)

RIDLEY, Jane, *Bertie: A Life of Edward VII* (Vintage, 2013)

ROBINSON, Jane, *Hearts and Minds: The Untold Story of the Great Pilgrimage and How Women Won the Vote* (Transworld, 2018)

SMITH, M.D., *Leverhulme's Rivington* (Amadells Press Ltd, 1998)

WINTERSON, Jeanette, *Courage Calls to Courage Everywhere* (Canongate Books, 2018)

Online Resources

Ancestry www.ancestry.co.uk

Lancashire Archives www.lancashire.gov.uk/libraries-and-archives/archives-and-record-office/

The UK Parliament www.parliament.uk

The British Library www.bl.uk

The History Press www.thehistorypress.co.uk

The National Archives www.nationalarchives.gov.uk

Friends of Winckley Square www.winckleysquarepreston.org

The UK Government www.gov.uk

The Obama Administration www.obamawhitehouse.archives.gov

Index